The Audacity to be a Writer

50 Inspiring Articles on Writing that Could Change Your Life

By Bryan Hutchinson, Joe Bunting, C.S. Lakin, Ali Luke, Marcy McKay, Shanan Haislip, Andy Mort, Christine Frazier, Liwen Ho, Chelsea Nenno, Claire DeBoer, The Magic Violinist, Josh Irby, Stacy Claflin, Nicole Gulotta, Dana Sitar and Bryan Collins

Visit the *Positive Writer* Blog

Founded by Bryan Hutchinson

www.PositiveWriter.com

*"**Stand by to be motivated!** Bryan Hutchinson's mission is to help fellow writers by inspiring them to put aside any uncertainties and be what they truly want to be – practicing writers."*

–Jonathan Gunson of *Bestseller Labs*

"Bryan Hutchinson's Positive Writer is as good as its name. In his ever-honest and ever-insightful articles, he offers positive motivation, inspiration, and encouragement to writers of all stripes and experience levels."

–K.M. Weiland of *Helping Writers Become Authors*

"Bryan's blog—Positive Writer—is exactly that: positive! The posts are full of encouragement and practical advice that can help every writer plow through rejection and waiting and disappointment and find joy in the writing journey. No wonder Positive Writer wins awards and is highly acclaimed. We all need a shot of "positive" to keep us going. Thanks so much, Bryan!"

–C. S. Lakin of *Live Write Thrive*

"Positive Writer is one of the Top Ten Blogs for Writers." (Award)

–Mary Jaksch, Editor-in-Chief of *Write to Done*

Writer's Doubt, the Book:

Also by Bryan Hutchinson and available on Amazon,

"If you struggle like I do with self-doubt, then this book has good news for you: you just might be a writer. Like a good friend, Bryan guides you through his own process of facing his inner demons, conquering the craft, and creating work that matters."

—**Jeff Goins**, author of *The Art of Work*

Table of Contents

Introduction

Thanks for picking up this compilation of articles on the magnificent art of writing. The articles selected for this book are the most popular blog posts from *Positive Writer* and many other bloggers blogging on the Craft of writing. **This entire collection of articles will never be available in one place again.**

This is not your typical book. The work is down-to-earth in a way that is refreshing, encouraging and ultimately, we hope, inspiring. I've always found blog articles to be an interesting and liberating form of writing (and reading). It's a casual form of writing, more akin to talking with a good friend over the backyard fence and, I'll be honest with you, I enjoy such freedom. I hope you do, too.

The blog posts were selected as a result of the number of online "views" and "social shares" they received. In a very real way, the readers picked the articles. The posts are presented as they first appeared online with only light editing for typos. Under the title of each article is the name of the author it is written by. Regular contributors to *Positive Writer* may have multiple articles included.

Part of the proceeds from this book will go towards supporting the *Positive Writer* website, our regular contests, giveaways and other events. In fact, if you visit *Positive Writer* today, you may be able to enter our latest writing contest, if one is currently running. If not, one will be starting soon. Feel free to subscribe to the blog to stay up-to-date and not miss out on anything.

Before we get to the articles, I want to wholeheartedly thank all of our guests who contributed:

Joe Bunting of *The Write Practice*, C.S. Lakin of *Live Write Thrive*, Ali Luke of *Aliventures*, Marcy McKay of *Mud Pie Writing*, Shanan Haislip of *The Procrastiwriter*, Andy Mort of *Sheep Dressed Like Wolves*, Christine Frazier of the *Better Novel Project*, Liwen Ho of *2square2behip*, Chelsea Nenno of *The Chelsea Page*, Claire DeBoer of *The Gift of Writing*, Kate Foley of *The Magic Violinist*, Josh Irby of *JoshIrby.com*, Stacy Claflin of *StacyClaflin.com*, Dana Sitar of *Writers Bucket List*, Nicole Gulotta of *Eat This Poem* and Bryan Collins of *Become a Writer Today*.

And thank you to: Jeff Goins, Jonathan Gunson, K.M. Weiland, and Joe Bunting for permission to republish guest articles I first published on their blogs.

Special thanks to my wife, Joan Faith. None of what I write ever gets published without her reading it first. She's my editor-in-chief in writing and everything else.

And most importantly, thank YOU. Thank you for being a writer. And thank you for caring about your Craft. You inspire me and all of the contributors in this book to do what we love to do, write. We hope our words help inspire you to write, too. And who knows? Maybe you'll read an article or two that inspires you in a way that changes your life, perhaps by helping you become a more confident writer.

— *Bryan Hutchinson*

The Audacity to be a Writer

By Bryan Hutchinson

You're a writer. An artist.

You write about things that matter to you and I'm sure you hope those things will matter to others, but even if they don't you're still going to do the work.

That's what artists do. It's remarkable. But it's more than that.

It's audacious. You don't need recognition and approval.

We might want it, and from time to time we may even wonder why we're not getting more of it, but we: Don't. Need. It.

Vincent van Gogh wasn't recognized as an artist during his lifetime, and yet today there's no argument that he was an artist. One of the greatest. Ever.

Van Gogh created art whether anyone cared or not. He didn't need recognition or the applauding approval of an audience. In fact, he only sold one painting during his lifetime, *The Red Vineyard*.

He didn't need you. He didn't need me.

He didn't need anyone to recognize his greatness.

All he needed were his canvases, brushes, and paint.

He was audacious like that.

That's remarkable. Really.

I'm sure when you think about it, you'll realize you don't need anyone's approval, or their recognition for that matter.

"I can do nothing about it if my paintings don't sell. The day will come, though, when people will see that they're worth more than the cost of the paint and my subsistence, very meager in fact, that we put into them." —Vincent van Gogh in a letter to his brother, Theo: Arles, c. 25 October 1888.

What's audacious about being a writer? You're a writer, regardless of whether anyone buys your work or not. It's the work itself that matters. You simply need the means to put your words on paper.

Being audacious is about taking risks, going against conventions and the status quo.

Trivial things like keeping up with the Joneses and the 9 to 5 lifestyle are not for you.

As writers, we battle inner turmoil every day caused by doubt, and we create work with no guarantees it will be accepted. In fact, there will be those who dislike it and harshly criticize it.

We give most of our lives to doing something no one fully understands, much less appreciates, except fellow artists who are also brave enough to create anyway.

That's audacious.

In a hundred years, whether you sell all of your work or only one piece – or none – all that will matter is that your words are still here.

Our words live on. So write. Scribble your little writer's heart out. Your work matters.

You're a writer. An artist. Indeed. You're audacious like that.

The Most Important Step You Can Take (for Your Writing Career)

By Bryan Hutchinson (Originally published on *Goins Writer*)

As long as I can remember, I've wanted to be a writer. But for one reason or another, I always put off the dream. I set it aside and allowed time to pass, doing things that seemed more important.

I neglected to take the most important step you can take in pursuing your dream: the first one. I built up excuses in my mind about opening myself up, not thinking anyone would want to read my words. But in reality, I was succumbing to the death knell of so many would-be writers. I was stalling because I didn't want to be exposed and rejected.

What does it take? This is the most common question I'm asked about writing a book, starting a blog, creating a network, or doing just about anything.

What's required? How do I do this? Will it be hard? The answer may be simpler than you think. It is the most critical ingredient to doing something that matters:

You've got to start.

Keep it simple, don't complicate the process, and don't over think it. Simply start somewhere, and where you are right now is probably as good a place as any.

Too many of us delay doing work that matters due to seemingly legitimate reasons. I did it for years. My fear of exposure made me constantly postpone taking the step that mattered most. The first one. I would tell myself, "I'm not a good writer." But I now understand that the message is more important than the level of quality I consider my writing to be.

I had to step past my insecurities and write anyway.

They did it: Stephen King, J.K. Rowling, Steve Jobs, Oprah Winfrey, and Seth Godin all started somewhere. And they all had work that was rejected.

Stephen King sold his first story, "The Glass Floor," for $35. It was a start. But the first novel that he completed, *The Long Walk*, was rejected. I've read that *Carrie* was rejected 30 times and Stephen finally gave up and threw it in the trash, but thankfully, his wife fished it out.

J.K. Rowling started writing *Harry Potter* while on a train, and she finished it using an old manual typewriter. Rowling was on welfare at the time and a divorced, single mother. Twelve publishing houses rejected *Harry Potter* before it finally found a publisher, and in 1997, Rowling received an £8000 grant from the Scottish Arts Council so she could carry on writing.

Steve Jobs famously started his first computer business in a garage with Steve Wozniak. Wozniak insists it actually all started in Jobs' bedroom, but what matters is they started somewhere. By the way, the computer they created was rejected by both HP and Atari. That's how Apple was born.

Oprah suffered an abusive childhood and watched television as her escape while dreaming of becoming famous. She started a broadcasting career at WVOL radio in Nashville. She later went on to television where she co-anchored a 6 o'clock news broadcast from which she was reportedly fired. Oprah started over again in morning television and eventually became the host of the #1 talk show on television for 24 seasons.

Seth Godin frequently talks about his failures. That's good news, because it also means he's started enough projects to fail over and over again and yet have major successes along the way. Seth has revealed that he has gotten 900 rejection letters from book publishers.

Now it's your turn…

Your work might get rejected, too, but even the best of the best get rejected. None of us are safe. Sooner or later we've got to take the step, dip our toes, or dive in.

Here's what you can do today:

1. Open your word processor.

2. Type a title for your book.

3. Write the first page.

It doesn't have to be perfect; it doesn't even have to be great. Simply start. Make it physical. Make it real. Keep in mind that whatever you write doesn't have to be published or shared with anyone. The only mission at hand is to write. Write freely and openly. Mix ideas to create a unique perspective.

And see what you end up with.

It's the starting that matters. I finally wrote my first book, a memoir about my childhood (*One Boy's Struggle*), at the age of 37. I had no plan, outline, or goal. No preconceived notions or dreams of grandeur. The only way I finally did it was that I came to the point that I was no longer concerned with whether I was a good writer or not, or if anyone would read my work or not.

Earlier this year, I gave away free review copies of my memoir on Story Cartel, and it became their second most downloaded book so far.

If we don't start, we'll never know what could be.

Publishing my memoir inspired me to start a blog, too, and I've reached people all over the world. Thanks to starting, I learned that I love to encourage people, especially those overwhelmed with doubt, as I was. Because of that, I've wanted to step out my original niche to reach even more people, but I put it off.

Maybe I didn't think I was good enough or was afraid of rejection. But then one fateful day, I took an important step and started a new blog I had only dreamed of but consistently delayed.

In only a few months, I received an award for the blog. Who knew? The point isn't just that I'm better than I gave myself credit for (although that's a good point, too). It's about starting anyway, regardless of what the results may be. Sometimes we need a push to get started — and that's okay. Maybe this will be that for you. I hope so.

2 Insanely Simple Steps for Becoming A REAL Writer

By Marcy McKay of *Mud Pie Writing*

Do you want to write? Silly question. Of course you do. You long to write. You dream of it. You crave words like chocolate. You're 100% dedicated to your craft.

However, you're not actually writing these days. Maybe you're still researching your subject matter. Or, you want to wait until your kids are older. You might plan to write full-time after retirement, when you have more time and money.

Maybe you're actually putting pen to paper every day, or are tapping away at your computer. At least you were.

You're taking time off to plot how to make the conflict bigger in your novel. Several agents rejected your last manuscript, and you're waiting to regroup. Deciding what's next.

These are all familiar reasons to not write. They're also...

Procrastination.

Excuses meant to keep you from living your dream. Tricks to trap you in wanna-be mode forever. Let's explore this deeper.

You Put the "Pro" in Procrastinate

Procrastination is the most common form of writer's block because it's so darn easy to rationalize. You don't say, "I'm never going to write my novel."

You say, "I'm going to write my novel. Tomorrow." Or, you only have 30 minutes to write, but you waste all that time on Twitter.

When you rip off the mask of procrastination, you discover the real culprit is that rat-bastard – Doubt. Doubt's #1 job is to keep you from writing.

Procrastination and Perfection

Perfectionism is often an excuse for procrastination.

Stop waiting for the ideal circumstances in your life to happen first. I don't know about you, but chaos is the norm around my house. Something's pretty much always broken, so there's always an unexpected bill to pay. My husband and I have two teenagers, so I'm usually worried about one, if not both, kids.

Enough with these white lies:

You don't need a $1,500 laptop to write. You don't need a degree to write. You don't need to be childless to write. All you need is the desire and determination to do so.

If you've tried to write before, but were less than pleased with the results, then congratulations! You're an honest-to-goodness writer. Real writing takes place later in the editing phase – the rewriting and reshaping of your words. Remember, anything worthwhile takes time, patience and practice.

Could you play Beethoven's Symphony Number Five on the first try? Could you run a marathon without training for a mile in the beginning? If I dropped you in Moscow today, could you speak Russian?

No, no, and no.

So, why do you think magic should flow from your fingers from day one? Why do you think your first draft should be a New York Times Bestseller? Why do you expect perfection?

Go Big or Go Home

It doesn't matter whether you're an introvert or extrovert. All writers have a dramatic side, or else you wouldn't want to write beautiful poems, wonderful short stories, or the great American novel.

Non-fiction can be just as powerful – a thought-provoking idea can become an overnight success.

If you keep thinking you can't write until blank happens, stop.

Stop right now. Quit thinking all-or-none. Stop believing you have to go BIG, or go home. There's a better way to accomplish more, while abusing yourself less.

2 Simple Steps for Writing Success

Many say they want to write, but few put those words into action. Try these two steps to move you from the couch to the computer:

1.   Name Your Procrastination

First, acknowledge your fear. Call it by name, so you know exactly who the enemy is. Be as specific as possible.

- I tell people I'm still researching my book, but the truth is I'm afraid to start writing. What if I have no talent?
- I stay up too late, eat junk food and watch reality TV every night. I oversleep the next day, and never write. I'm sabotaging myself.
- I don't have time to sit down, and really focus on writing like I want. I don't care what that stupid post said -- now isn't the best time for me.

2. Small Steps

Big, sweeping change is too much, too soon. It terrifies you, and throws you back into procrastination mode. Think tiny, baby steps.

- I've researched enough. After the kids go to bed, I'm going to start writing one hour, at least three nights per week.
- I'm going to throw away all my junk food. No more eating after 7 p.m. I'm going to bed by 10 p.m., so I can start writing by 6 a.m. I'd like to write for one hour before my family wakes up.
- I don't have as much time as I'd like, but I want to write just 250 words per day. That's just one page and doable. Hopefully, I'll move on, but I can commit to 250.

Writing every day is best, but do the best you can. It's also okay if you still procrastinate sometimes. We all do (Facebook is my time waster of choice), but I try to use that as reward to work first, then social media later.

Keep trying until you find what works for you. Everyone has a different creative process, but we all write the same way.

One word at a time.

A Crazy Myth Writers Need to Kill

By Bryan Hutchinson

When I was in my early twenties and an up and coming pool player, I thought in order to be the best, I needed to know everything about billiards. I thought I needed to know how the tables were made, what the balls were made of, and even the ins and outs of cue design.

Then one day while in the pool room, sitting in a lounge chair "reading" a book on how to make billiard tables, my mentor tapped me on the shoulder and snapped me out of a daydream. Truth was, I had drifted off because the book was boring and I wasn't really interested in building tables.

"Why are you reading that?" he asked, and I told him. What he said next was life-changing.

My mentor was a champion and one of the best money players in the country. "Listen, Bryan, if you try and explain to me the mechanics of how to put spin on the balls, I'll tune you out. I don't need to understand it from a technical perspective. I just need to be able to use it. I know how to use it because I feel it. Because I'm a pool player."

His words blew my mind and completely changed what I thought I knew about becoming a professional player. It made me reconsider something I had believed and thus lifted self-imposed restraints I had created in my mind.

Over the following years of playing pool, I dominated players who knew every aspect of the game much better than I could ever hope to, the mechanics, the terminology and the history... and, of course, there were players who were extremely knowledgeable of those things who beat me.

I became a professional player because I knew how to play the game, not that I totally understood it in a technical sense, but because I spent countless hours at the table hitting the balls and practicing.

I could feel the game.

Even now, players still mention jargon about pool that baffles me, and yet when I tell them they've lost me, they give me a shocked look and say something like, "You must know! I've seen you use it!" But I don't. Not the way they do.

So, predictably, they determine I must learn it *their way* and go into a long discourse about the topic at hand, explaining every little aspect of it. If only they'd stuck a needle in my eye, it would've been far less painful.

So what does this have to do with writing?

If you're like me and you have difficulty remembering jargon, or the difference between such terms as adjectives and adverbs, you're not a lost cause. You're still a writer.

Simply because some people tell you that you need to know everything about writing doesn't mean you need to know *everything*, at least not the way they do. If you buy into such assertions, Writer's Doubt will eat you up and spit you out.

Similarly to playing pool and winning games against more knowledgeable players, I've sold thousands more books than authors who understand writing in a way I never will. And, of course, there are countless authors who have a more complete understanding of writing who have sold tons more than I have. There's nothing wrong with either of these realities.

The Myth:

You need to be an expert in all aspects of writing to be a writer.

No, you don't.

You don't need to be an expert in all aspects of writing to be a writer.

You don't need to be a grammar master, you don't need to know everything about punctuation, and you don't need to be able to teach English 101. Sure, it's great if you can, but it's not necessary.

Stephen King vs. Danielle Steel

Stephen King graduated from the University of Maine at Orono in 1970, with a B.A. in English and qualified to teach it in school. He published his first novel, *Carrie,* in 1974. King has sold over 350 million copies of his books so far.

Danielle Steel never studied writing in school. She published her first novel, *Going Home,* in 1973. Steel is the fourth bestselling author of all time and the bestselling author alive today, with over 800 million copies of her books sold so far.

In an interview, Danielle Steel was asked:

Q: Did you study writing in school?

A: *No, never did... Who knows, maybe I missed out on something important – then again, maybe not!*

(Interview: July 2004 by Rosanne L., Matthews Branch Library)

What do Charles Dickens, Mark Twain, Jack London, George Bernard Shaw, and H.G. Wells all have in common?

They all dropped out of school very young and were uneducated writers in the traditional sense. However, let me be clear, I believe education is important. I mention the above authors to make a point:

As a writer, there's only ONE thing you need to be able to do: write.

What I have discovered is this: there's no right way or wrong way to be a writer. Some people have a great technical knowledge of writing, while others don't. You need to do what works *for you*.

If you have difficulty remembering all the technical terms in writing, but you can write like there's no tomorrow and have a good feeling for how it should be, who's to tell you that you need to know and understand all of the jargon?

Of course, I am biased because I have difficulty remembering terminology and definitions, and frankly, it ticks me off because I'd really like to remember, but that doesn't stop me from writing and publishing.

Maybe there's something about writing, or whatever your art might be, that doesn't fit your style or the way your brain works, and when you try to force yourself to conform, you get stuck?

Here's what I would like to ask of you:

If something is causing you to stall, take another look at it and ask yourself, do you really need it? If it's stopping you from creating your art, maybe it's time to reconsider it and create anyway.

Whether you're traditionally educated in writing like Stephen King, or have never studied writing in school like Danielle Steel, you can be a writer!

So do us all a favor and write. Because you are a writer!

Just as you must kill your darlings, you must kill the myths that hold you back from writing. Don't let the dreaded Writer's Doubt overwhelm you into submission. You can overcome it!

*I've received several emails asking about "Kill your darlings." My inspiration was from a phrase made famous by William Faulkner, "In writing, you must kill all your darlings." It refers to the dangers of a writer using favorite elements that might confuse the reader. However, if you like trivia, the phrase originated from Arthur Quiller-Couch, who spread it in his 1913-1914 Cambridge lectures *On the Art of Writing*, "Whenever you feel an impulse to perpetrate a piece of exceptionally fine writing, obey it whole heartedly and delete it before sending your manuscript to press. Murder your darlings."

Why You are Not Finishing the Writing You Started

By Shanan Haislip of *The Procrastiwriter*

Are you the kind of writer who's brimming with ideas, but can't seem to finish a single one of them?

That was me. I had a ton of ideas, and they sounded great for a paragraph, maybe a page, but then they'd just… fade. My work-in-progress would inevitably be consigned to a bottom drawer, never to be finished.

All of my ideas seemed doomed to fail. In fact, my inability to finish work was making me doubt myself as a writer. Until one day, I pitched an idea to a magazine, and it was accepted. Cue panic. Now what?

Not having the option to quit taught me a huge lesson: The problem wasn't my ideas, it was how I handled them once they appeared.

Inspiration: *I was doing it wrong.*

Here's what I learned about ideas, and how to make them stick around for the long haul.

1. Let the Idea Breathe

I'm an ignoramus about wine, but I married into a family that's very knowledgeable about it. The one concept I struggled with was the idea of uncorking a bottle of red wine, and then just… leaving it there. On the counter. "You have to let it breathe," I was told.

Letting wine "breathe," whatever that meant, seemed grandly silly. It's wine, I thought. You're supposed to drink it, not stare at it.

However you feel about letting wine breathe (I'm still not sold on that), the concept is a useful way to think about your ideas. If you get struck with inspiration, and rush to your desk to write it down, that's like uncorking new wine and drinking it straight away.

Instead, start writing around it. Freewrite about it. Ask your idea questions. Get to know your thoughts about the topic. Write your last sentence. Cross it out. Write another one.

Whatever you do, get to know your idea before diving straight into Chapter 1.

2. Write Your Idea's Elevator Speech

Consciously or unconsciously, there's an endgame, a point, to your idea. In the case of the piece I pitched to the writing magazine, it was: Every writer is a musician, whether they realize it or not.

Can you find that kind of nugget in your idea? Something that has to be proven, has to be shared? Imagine writing the query letter that's going to accompany this idea. What would the first paragraph say? Write it down. When momentum starts to slip, stare at it. Get passionate again. Keep writing.

3. Put Your Idea On a Deadline

A deadline makes me wiggle out from under the rock of "someday," reminds me I can't quit writing when it's difficult, and forces me to finish what I start.

Fortunately, deadline-driven writing opportunities are everywhere. Sending query letters, pitching an article to a magazine, an essay to a literary journal, or a book to an agent, puts you on a deadline. The secret is to complete steps 1 and 2 above, and start querying while your idea is still bright and shiny.

If your inquiry gets accepted, you'll probably have that moment of panic, like I did. What do I do now?

You'll write, rewrite, stare out a lot of windows, and chew on a lot of pens (just me?). You might write a few drafts. My magazine pitch took seven drafts before I considered it finished.

And you know what? You'll figure it out.

7 Distractions Stopping You from Writing (and How to Beat Them!)

By Andy Mort of *Sheep Dressed Like Wolves*

Whether you are a professional, doing it alongside a day job, or it's simply a hobby, you write because you feel a compulsion. It's a passion, a calling, a process that brings you to life and helps you make sense of the world.

But simply loving something doesn't make it easy to do. I think Dorothy Parker connected with a deep and collective truth when she said:

"I hate writing, I love having written."

It feels good to step back and observe something I have spent my time creating and crafting.

It's a wonderful feeling to have written, in large part because writing is not easy. The doubts, confusion, and endless potential can make for an overwhelming foundation from which to start each time.

We bring a lot of baggage to the table, which can make us forget that although it's not easy, writing IS quite simple...You just have to start.

Only, it's the starting that hurts, isn't it?

We get distracted and convince ourselves of reasons why we are not quite ready to do the work.

But if we are going to get to that beautiful place at the end of the day, the happy land of "Having Written," we must recognize the road blocks we put in our own way.

There are many things that stop me from starting. Here are just seven of them:

1. Reading ABOUT Writing

I spend a lot of time reading motivational blog posts and books about creativity and "doing the work." So much time, in fact, that it became an evident irony when every time I sat down to write, I picked up *The War of Art* by Steven Pressfield, *You are a Writer* by Jeff Goins, or *Writer's Doubt* by Bryan Hutchinson.

I was inspired, but remained completely passive and creatively paralyzed. So I had to ration my consumption of these materials. I don't look at my RSS feed, social networks, or email updates until I've written for at least an hour (usually two) each morning.

2. Obsessing Over Routine

I also fall prey to Routine Envy. I love to read about the daily routines of my heroes, and spend a lot of time pondering ways to imitate them. Or at least I did, until I had a conversation with someone who was thinking of emulating MINE. It seemed ridiculous, and at that point, I realized that no one has the perfect routine; we all just experiment with how we mix what we want to do with the time we have available to do it.

Find your rhythm and patterns that work for you, but don't stress about it and don't obsess over getting it perfect. You never will. Just decide what you want to do (write) and unearth time every day to do it.

3. Comparing Yourself to Others

Do you ever look with envy through the lens of social media at the lives of others who appear to be doing what you want to be doing?

Again, you learn an important lesson when you realize there are people looking at you in exactly the same way. We are all muddling along, learning, and making things up as we go along.

We all have messy and confusing insides that we compare with the outward projections of others.

4. Developing Strategic Quick Fixes

Another thing I tend to do when I sit down to write is to search for quicker ways to achieve results. Formulas, outlines, and paint-by-numbers solutions to writing. And judging by Google's most searched for terms, many people are on the lookout for similar things.

Structure is obviously extremely useful when it comes to writing, but again I find my search for quicker ways to work can distract me from actually doing the writing. If you want to work with an outline then develop a very simple one and commit to sticking with it for a while.

5. Feeling Sorry for Yourself

There are times when I don't start writing because I'm doing nothing other than feeling sorry for myself, doubting every choice I've ever made, and wondering what the hell I'm thinking trying to write words for people to read. These are the moments I allow every critical thing anyone has ever said to enter my mind and the doubts to niggle me to a place of inaction.

I have a specific mailbox where I put encouraging emails from people who have experienced transformation because of a message I happened to pen. When I feel tempted to stop writing because I want to wallow in my own self-doubt, I remind myself of the bigger picture. My work is not about me and my self-pity or self-indulgence.

Some days we are just empty. I find there are times when I need to step away from the screen and do something that nourishes my soul and fills you back up. Otherwise I resent my creative process and have nothing left to give.

Identify the difference between your emptiness and your fear-fuelled block.

6. Researching Yourself into Oblivion

Do you ever think to yourself, "I'll be ready to write once I know what I'm talking about," and then proceed to lose yourself in articles, videos, and books about the subject you want to write on? I often find myself so overwhelmed that I completely lose perspective of what I set out to create initially.

Focus Focus Focus.

7. Waiting for Inspiration to Strike

This is an obvious one and to some extent it encapsulates procrastination in a nutshell. As a writer who takes the craft seriously, you must turn pro in your mind before you turn pro in your "reality."

For me, the biggest difference between the pro mindset and the mind of an amateur is in our relationship with inspiration. The amateur creates when they're inspired; the pro goes to work in order to get inspired. In other words...they start. You'll read these words from many of the best writers of today and yesterday.

"Having Written" is a great feeling. It's a beautiful destination. But if you don't actually step off the platform you will never get there, however much it looks to others and yourself like your intention is to catch the train. No writer feels adequate, ready, or distraction-free enough to start. Yet we must.

How to Become a Better Writer

By Bryan Hutchinson

Every writer wants the process of writing to be easy. We want our writing to pour forth, as if from an inexhaustible reservoir. We all want our first and only drafts to become bestsellers. And we want our readers to not only get us, but to never get enough of us. When we show up for readings, Madison Square Garden won't be big enough to hold all of our loyal fans.

Deep down inside, we know what we really-really want. We all want to become bestselling authors. We might not all be ready to admit this, and that's okay. That's all well and good, but before that happens, before the bright lights and throngs of readers eager to get your autograph show up, there's something every writer on God's green earth must come to terms with:

Writing is hard work and must be done daily.

A writer doesn't only write when motivated. A writer doesn't only write when inspired. And a writer most certainly doesn't only write when the muse pays a visit. The muse is far too fickle, so stop waiting for it.

If we're willing to admit it (I raise my hand), at some point we all have dreams of writing the next blockbuster, such as the next *Da Vinci Code* by Dan Brown, or the next *The Shining* by Stephen King, or the next *The Gift* by Danielle Steel, but not every writer is willing to put his or her butt in the chair and write every-single-day.

You have an important story to tell, and no one can tell it but you. But writing every now and then, only when the urge comes to you, when you feel inspired, or especially motivated, isn't enough.

A writer must discipline herself to write every day, rain or shine, inspiration or no inspiration – good, bad, or ugly. That's how we become better writers, by writing every day. (And that's what I've struggled with. Maybe you have, too?)

What do Stephen King, Daniel Steel, and Dan Brown have in common?

Bestselling authors Stephen King, Daniel Steel, and Dan Brown do not simply show up whenever they feel good and ready and write merely on a whim. That's not how it works. They write every day, whim or no whim.

Stephen King sets out each day with a quota of 2000 words and will not stop writing until it is met.

"Read and write four to six hours a day. If you cannot find the time for that, you can't expect to become a good writer." —Stephen King

Danielle Steel writes for 20 hours a day while writing four or five books at the same time.

"I eventually sit down to write the book, and when I do that I pretty much lock myself up for about a month and do only that for about 20 hours a day. I'm usually working on four or five books at once." —Danielle Steel

At least Dan Brown remembers to take breaks. He writes 7 days a week, beginning at sunrise, with an antique hour glass on his desk to remind him to take hourly exercise breaks.

"If I'm not at my desk by sunrise, I feel like I'm missing my most productive hours." —Dan Brown

The Power of Inspiration

It's great to feel inspired to write, but the power of inspiration alone does not create a writer. Writing creates a writer.

If you want to write that book you've been meaning to write: Start writing, every day.

I've found that it helps to have a personal quota. Consider creating a fixed number of words to write each day, and don't stop writing until you've met your quota (or more), perhaps 500 words as Hemingway did, or 2000 words as Stephen King writes per day. Of course, it's up to you how many words you write, but whatever you do: Write. Every. Day.

4 Pieces of Well-meaning Writing Advice to Beware of

By Shanan Haislip

Writers get well-meaning advice all the time. Whether you're a poet, a novelist, a business writer, or the editor of *The New York Times*, there will always be people telling you how to do what you do, but this way. Their way.

Should you always listen? Good question.

Write What You Know

I don't know about you, but I have lived a basically pleasant, average life. I believe everyone gets dealt their measure of unhappiness and discord, but I was never abducted by Somali pirates, I've never contracted a rare disease, traveled the world, had a whirlwind love affair with the son of a minor European royal, or even gone skydiving.

What if what you know is kind of boring? Does that mean you're a pretentious try-hard for wanting to do more than that? Should you feel under qualified?

No. Writing what you don't know means you'll have to do some research, so be sure to put yourself in a teachable frame of mind. Get ready to learn. But, please, for the benefit of modern literature, feel free to write about that which you don't know.

Only Pretentious Smartypants Use Semicolons

A variation of this advice is famously attributed to Kurt Vonnegut: "Here is a lesson in creative writing. First rule: Do not use semicolons. They are transvestite hermaphrodites representing absolutely nothing. All they do is show you've been to college."

Kurt, I beg to differ.

First, you need not have been to college to understand how a semicolon works and second, sometimes, nothing else will do when you want to tie two corresponding-yet-complete thoughts together in a melodious way. The most common (non-listing) way to use a semicolon is to bind two independent clauses (word-blobs with complete subject-and-predicate structures) together.

Turn a deaf ear to any and all writing advice that tries to take tools out of your writing toolbox and tries to tell you that it's for your own good.

Never End a Sentence with a Preposition

At one point, I was a holier-than-thou writing tutor, and I had one commandment. Never, ever, under any circumstances, end a sentence with a word like to, for, from, in or with. I would always make my students bury these words further down in earlier parts of the sentence, confident that I was properly apprenticing them in the art of wordsmithing.

Too bad I didn't realize that the prepositions rule included other, longer words like between, beyond, upon, and about. I'm sure we can all think of beautiful, perfectly literary ways to use these words to end sentences, and more importantly, Grammar Girl says it's okay, and so does Merriam-Webster.

Show, Don't Tell

Before you crucify me, let me say that 99% of the time, "Show, don't tell," is a perfectly necessary piece of advice that all writers, particularly those new to the craft, need to heed religiously. Too much telling is almost invariably boring. New writers think that telling feels to the reader like the training montage from Rocky; actually, it usually feels like having to sit through a story that usually ends with, "Guess you had to be there."

For experienced writers, nonfiction writers especially, acclaimed essayist Philip Lopate has a rebuttal to this advice. In his writing advice guide *To Show and To Tell: The Craft of Literary Nonfiction*, Lopate says, "The nonfiction student's reluctance to provide summary and analysis shows the markings of that nefarious taboo of writing programs everywhere: "Show, don't tell."... We must rely on the subjective voice of the narrator to guide us, and if that voice never explains, summarizes or interprets... we are in big trouble."

It's fine to use telling as the connective tissue that binds your scenes together and provides crucial information.

You can waste half a page of context clues for the reader to guess Mama's age, or you could tell us she's 37. It's up to you, and sometimes, it's better not to waste the space. Conclusion? Tell—sometimes.

What Michelangelo Taught Me about Writer's Doubt

By Christine Frazier of the _Better Novel Project_ (This post won first place in Positive Writer's "Writer's Doubt" writing contest.)

When there's a giant obstacle blocking me from my desk chair, it's always the same question: Why did I think I could be a writer? It's worse than writer's block, a missing muse, or even the inner critic – because sometimes I don't even make it far enough for those other hurdles to step in.

This is Writer's Doubt: self-sabotage and fear that burrows so deep inside of me, so thoroughly, that I don't know what's real and what's not.

But there's one thing I do know that's real, and it's a moment that I turn to again and again– the moment I saw Michelangelo's sculptures in Florence, The Unfinished Slaves.

"I saw the angel in the marble and I carved until I set him free." – Michelangelo

You see, I had traveled to Italy to take it all in– the art, the cafés, the charm– and I expected this to magically fuel beautiful writing.

When it wasn't that easy, I just felt very, very lonely. And loneliness breeds doubt. I questioned why I was standing in line to see Michelangelo's David instead of working on my story. After all, by the time I made it to the Gallery Accademia, I had already seen David's body on souvenir barbecue aprons, his [ahem] on novelty condom wrappers, not to mention the actual full-size replica in the piazza.

But, I had to see the David just so I could say so. And like I said, I was lonely. It felt good to go through the motions of the experience I thought I should be having. After an hour in line, I came to terms with what a phony I was because I just. didn't. care.

And then, before I made it to the David, I saw the most beautiful artwork I've ever had the honor of standing in front of. There was no crowd or line waiting to see these massive hunks of unpolished stone: *The Prisoners, The Slaves, The Unfinished Ones*.

I gazed up at the prisoners in the marble: Larger-than-life men, half-fighting their stone cages, half-content to die there. Michelangelo knew how to dig them out. All he had to do was hammer in the right places— just like all we writers have to do is put one word after another.

These sculptures pierced through my loneliness and self-doubt, and I was left with a whisper stuck in my lungs— I was overwhelmed with the contrast of these crude blocks and the angels he found inside of them. All Michelangelo had to do was clear away the muck. With each clink clink clink of his chisel, he cleared away the to-do lists, the self-doubt, and guilt of doing what he wanted.

"If you knew how much work went into it, you would not call it genius." —Michelangelo

And the instant I accepted that Michelangelo found these creatures inside of him, which let him find their forms in the marble, I remember the work.

Michelangelo was commissioned to make 40 of these giants. He failed. He only began a handful of them. Chiseling marble isn't like blowing the seeds off a dandelion, after all. It's work. The genius part is continuing the work, knowing somewhere inside of you that the creature is there, whether it be Atlas Slave or the hero of your novel. Michelangelo taught me that the trick is holding on.

These sculptures are always described as *non finiti.* Unfinished. These stone gods didn't make Michelangelo famous, but he did them anyway. They seem like an afterthought leading up the hallway to the David, but maybe they are the practice that made the David all the better. Or maybe he left them unfinished just to catch a lonely writer off guard.

So, there I was, standing in awe– not in the beauty of a perfectly finished product, but of the work and the process. And at that moment, the rays of these ideas converged and I felt them all: the inevitability of finding the forms, the work, and the beautiful failure.

I was moved. My planes of understanding moved, and I felt it all at once and separately at the same time. For a moment, art was faith, and understanding that concept was art in itself, too.

It was a moment that had the clarity usually reserved for falling asleep that can never be recalled– a spiritual kind of moment, even if I never knew how to describe spiritual before.

There is no doubt.

This then, is the moment that I have tucked in the folds of my mind. And still ten years after viewing these statues, I get a little teary-eyed as I remember how they looked– no– as I remember how I felt. To feel such a strong reaction to another's art work– You can't feel like that and walk away.

This is the moment that I pull up when I question my decision to pursue a creative life and to call myself a writer. When Writer's Doubt keeps my butt from planting in the chair, this is what I reach for.

And if a brief flash of this memory can turn into just five minutes more of overcoming Writer's Doubt, that's enough. Suddenly it's like looking at my doubt from far away, and it seems silly and obvious— just chisel it away.

So I urge you, if you've got that capacity to experience art (you do), to be moved in this deep way, and to feel beauty, then there is no doubt that you are on the right path. This is worth it.

Find that sentence in a book that makes you in awe of humankind, remember that film that leaves you speechless and quiet while the credits run, or remember the sculptures, sitting ignored in a hallway in Florence, pushing you forward.

And with that moment in hand, there is no doubt.

The Monster

By Liwen Ho of *2square2behip* (This post won second place in Positive Writer's "Writer's Doubt" writing contest)

You know how under every kid's bed is a monster? Well, I'll let you in on a little secret. In every writer's head exists a monster, too. I'm talking about that hairy, slimy, and drooling creature that taps you on the shoulder with its sharp claws as you type.

It's the one that snarls and stares down at you with its two – or three – googly eyes when you finish a blog post, an article, or a book. It's the monster that was conceived in a corner of your mind, then grew and grew to the point that it began crowding out all the good thoughts in your head.

Do you recognize this monster yet?

If not, let me introduce it to you. The monster hiding in every writer's head is called DOUBT. And boy, is it scary. It's scary enough to stop me in my tracks before I even get a single word written down. It's big enough to make me want to scrap whatever I'm working on and start over.

It's real enough to steal the joy from what I love to do the most – to write and to share my writing with others. I've already had plenty of opportunities in my short time as a writer to practice taming this monster. And what I've learned is:

This monster only has as much power over me as I give it. I can choose to cower in front of my laptop while it stomps around in my head, or I can decide to look it in the eyes, stick my tongue out at it, and prove it wrong.

I think the latter choice is more fun, don't you?

However, I've been having a harder time taming my monster lately, not because I haven't been able to write, but because I have finished writing. I am happy-overjoyed-to say I have completed my first novel. When I added the final period to the final sentence of the final chapter of my book, I was ready to cry and dance and shout from the rooftops. I wanted to stick my hands on my hips and say, "Take that!" to my monster for every moment it made me doubt during this whole process of writing.

But the next day while I was telling my girlfriend about finally being able to publish the book and she asked, "So I'll be able to buy it and read it on my Kindle?" my monster stood up again and knocked me over with its scaly tail.

"Uh, yes, but you don't have to read it," I replied with Writer's Doubt coursing through every cell in my body. Is it strange that I've worked so hard on my book, can't wait to publish it, but don't want anyone to read it? (I hope I'm not the only one with weird thoughts like this!)

Sure, my monster is trying to mess with my head (and heart) again, but I know it's doing so in part to protect me from getting hurt. It understands that putting my work out there for anyone and everyone to read can be risky.

It knows how hard it is to self-publish and market a book on your own. It wants to save me from the criticisms and rejections I will likely get. But these are 3 things that I'm trying to remind my monster, that monster called DOUBT, when it starts to act out:

1. *Not everyone will like or agree with my writing and (gulp!) it's* okay.

2. *My writing doesn't have to be perfect.*

3. *Growing as a writer takes time and each opportunity is a stepping stone to the next one.*

So, I hope my monster starts listening and having FAITH in what I'm telling it.

I will likely have to spend a lot of time with it in order to calm it down, but maybe that's what my monster needs, someone like Boo who was able to befriend Sulley and Mike in the movie *Monsters, Inc.* If she could make nice with some monsters, perhaps I can, too.

How to Overcome Self-Doubt

By Chelsea Nenno of _The Chelsea Page_ (This post won third place in Positive Writer's "Writer's Doubt" writing contest.)

How do you overcome Writer's Doubt?

You Start. Sit down and write. Stop Googling everyone who is already doing something. Don't read any more "how-to" writing books. No more stalking your competition.

Just Write.

Since six years old I knew I was a writer. Filling up blank pages and writing fiction stories in that old pink little journal. Unfortunately, somewhere along the way I was told I wasn't good enough. I was told that I didn't have what it took.

How was I told?

By those red script marks on each of my papers as they were criticized and critiqued. I was corrected in sentence structure and description. I was told "nice try" and told to move on.

The red marks were not only written on my paper. They were written on my heart. What I really wanted to be ended up being thrown under the rug. I was embarrassed I didn't have what it took to be a writer. I mean, that's what all those red marks were all about, right?

So the secret stayed within myself. I loved writing.

I've had journals since nine years old, hiding my secret instead of speaking them aloud. I dreamt of becoming an author. Day-dreamed of writing for magazines and publishers across the country.

Then I grew up.

With every job I participated in, I was always finding ways to incorporate my writing. But they were never welcomed ideas. Yet again, my words were pushed aside and that red marker made permanent marks on my heart.

I threw the dream away. I finally believed that those red marks marked the truth about me. I had no potential with words. Everyone else was better. Everyone else read everyone else. No one was interested in what I had to say. I was worthless. Useless. And the big one: *not good enough*.

Until recently. The dream came awake from hiding deep in my soul. I closed my eyes and let the day-dreaming begin. Tears flowed down my cheeks as I welcomed the feelings of excitement and inspiration flooded over me in the hopes that maybe, just maybe, this dream was really part of who I was made to be.

I sat up from my bed and took in a deep breath. I was bracing myself for the slap in the face I knew was coming. I was sure this was just a fantasy suffocating me from the responsible adult world that I needed to participate in.

To my surprise, healing words washed over me. I was listening to an interview of my favorite author, and she gave us the advice her professor in college told her. "Never, ever, stop writing." I sighed in relief, opened my journal, and put those words down.

Never, ever, stop writing!

It was then that I began to write. Really write. Not just in my journal. I finally allowed myself to finish writing the fiction I started when I was twelve years old. I began following blogs that inspired me to write. I looked for writing communities. And I started to ask for feedback that would help me, not hinder me.

My first blogs posts held encouraging comments from writing classmates that said I was funny! They even said they were looking forward to what I'd write next!

Whaaaat?!

This was healing for me. Not the comments in themselves, but the ability to write without fear of what people were going to say. All I had to do was put it out there confidently.

One of the bloggers that I follow wrote a post that told me something incredible. He said "Introduce yourself as a writer. It will change your life." So, I started writing it out.

My name is Chelsea, and I am a writer.

The next month, I quit my job. Not because I was making good income. No, not at all. But because I knew where I wanted to be and realized I had been killing my dream due to thinking I didn't have talent or ability.

I will not live my life in that lie anymore. Every day, there is a point where you have to accept yourself for who you really are. Not the person people expect you to be. But as the person you know you are deep in your soul.

Are you a writer? Then believe it!

I had to stop thinking about those red marks, and whether or not people were disgusted by my jumbled paragraphs. I had to stop remembering all the time that the writer I thought sucked had made the A+ list. Every day, I have to remember that I have my own voice, my own opinions, my own perspective. I'm different. You're different.

And some people need to hear it. Not from anyone else but YOU. We are not responsible for another person's happiness. We are responsible for ours. I had almost killed my dream of being a writer by allowing other people's perspectives of success to tell me I'd never arrive.

Now, I don't care! A lot of people will dislike what I write. Their words have the potential to cut me at the core. Yet, I know now that this is me. This is where I'm supposed to be.

Let's not forget why we love writing. It's not about the money. It's about the calling.

Writing is a calling! One that you have to accept for yourself. You know if you're called or not. If you're not, then get out of here and find your true passion! If you are, you can feel that burning in your heart, that excitement in your belly, and that thrill in your mind that dreams really do come true.

Just Write. Believe it, and do it.

3 Myths that Hold Your Best Writing Back

By Bryan Hutchinson

The odds are if you write in public, you want people to read your work. Seems like a reasonable assumption. I mean, if we don't care if anyone's reading our work, then we should stick to personal journals that we keep hidden under our pillows.

You can hide your work if you want to, and if you hide your work you'll never let yourself down. But if you're interested in getting your work noticed, try not to fall for the myths presented here.

Here's the thing: A lot of us who start out writing, blogging, and publishing go through the torturous phase of worrying about why "no one is paying attention to me."

In other words, we're writing our hearts out, giving everything we've got, and putting ourselves out there on the world's grandest stage (the internet)... and no one seems to care.

Crickets.

I've been there, and honestly, it sucks.

Every writer eventually comes to a crossroads, and when we reach it, we have to make a decision. Nothing short of your writing future is at stake. Either we decide to stop writing or we decide to press on and do whatever we need to improve, such as:

1. Take blogging / writing courses.

2. Hire a mentor / coach.

3. Follow and learn from the best bloggers and writers in your niche. (This is the easiest, and everyone should be doing it.)

4. Hone your focus.

5. Whatever you do, don't fall for the 3 most common myths. We'll get to those in a moment.

Or, as most people do, we try to avoid the decision and do something in the middle, and it's this middle that is the most dangerous, because it can be worse than merely quitting. The middle is where people lower their expectations and their standards, and as a result, their passion for writing begins to slowly die a torturous death.

The middle is where artists, like you and me, begin to tell ourselves that it's okay not to attract an audience and to not be noticed; it's okay that no one seems to care. And you know what? We don't need them anyway. After all, we need to be true to ourselves, and if we're not true to ourselves, then we shouldn't be doing this. Right?

But, unfortunately, the middle is not where people stay true to themselves. It's quite the opposite, in fact, and the longer one stays in the middle mindset (which is what it is, a mindset), the longer lower expectations and giving less than we've got to give take root and become our new normal. You don't want to be in the middle.

"Walk on road, hmmmmmm? Walk left side, safe. Walk right side, safe. Walk middle, sooner or later get squished just like grape." –Mr. Miyagi, from the movie, *Karate Kid*

You don't ever want to tell yourself it's okay that no one reads or cares about your work. It's not okay. When you come to the crossroads, it's a call to arms, it means it's time to up your game, become a better writer, and earn the attention your work deserves.

We're all better than we think we are, and we all have much more to offer than we think we do. And just when you think it's time to give up and go home, that, my friends, is when you've reached the crossroads.

Myth #1

It's okay to just write for myself. (But you write publicly on a blog and/or publish books.)

This is a simple, but not so effective, myth too many writers believe in to make themselves feel better about not attracting an audience.

Reality: If you're not attracting an audience, then you need to do something, change something, learn something, or be more audacious or even, less audacious.

Whatever you do, don't shrug your shoulders and say it's okay. You don't believe that and neither do I. Your writing deserves better. You deserve better.

Myth #2

What works for others should work for me.

This one used to drive me nuts! It's not true.

Reality: What works for others probably won't work for you. At least, not the exact same way or with the exact same results. That's why...

You have to be uniquely you. As with myth #1, you must find that "something" that works for you. It can be a variation of things others are doing, but you absolutely must make what you do your own.

How many singing competitions have you watched on TV and heard the judges tell contestants that the cover they did sounded copycatish? And then the judges follow up telling the artists to own the songs and make them their own. It's the same concept for writers.

Whatever you write about, whether it's for your blog or your next book, make it your own, make it uniquely yours, and own it.

And that's how you find your voice. You'll never find your voice by copying what works for others.

The real question is: What works for you?

Myth #3

Always give readers what they want.

Reality: Take risks and refuse to be predictable. Too many writers are playing it safe, and they're failing.

"People don't know what they want until you show it to them." – Steve Jobs

Stop trying to give readers what you think they want and give them something they don't know they want. Say what needs to be said. Say what only you can say— the way only you would say it. Be authentic. Stand out.

Your readers don't want to be pacified, and the odds are if you say what you believe, your readers will respect you for your honesty, even if some disagree with you. And you might be surprised when readers comment, "It's about time someone said it like it is!"

"If I had asked people what they wanted, they would have said faster horses." —Henry Ford

And what if you do write something that doesn't connect and your readers ignore it? Get back to work and keep improving. Your best work is ahead of you. Keep at it. Don't squander your gift. But remember, say something that matters, not something so watered down that people will nod their heads and then forget about you. Say it with conviction. Be different, and then get out of the way.

What can you write that differentiates you from everyone else?

The answer should be obvious. But it's not, and I don't know what the answer is for you. However, ask yourself, what do you want to say but you'd never dare say it for fear of embarrassment and /or shame, or it might make you look bad or cause people to disagree with you?

Think about it. You've got what it takes.

A lot of the times the answer is simple and closer than we think. And sometimes the answer has less to do with what you say and more to do with how you say it.

Earnest Vincent Wright wrote the novel, "Gadsby," which contained over 50,000 words and none of them with the letter E!

Do you know what the most-used letter in the English alphabet is? It's the letter E.

Every other blogger and just about anyone with an opinion can, and probably will, tell you what you should or shouldn't do to get your writing noticed. But guess what? None of that matters. It's all about you. Be revolutionary. Be you. And, let me be honest, by no means is writing in public easy. It's not.

Anyone can start a blog, or write and publish a book, and many thought that's all they needed to do to get noticed and attract an audience. Now you know it's not that easy.

9 Ways to Promote Your Writing without Being a Jerk

By Bryan Hutchinson

I bet you've heard (real or imagined) that self-promotion is creepy, despicable, and well, just plain wrong. Don't do it. How dare you even consider it?! Don't! And two stamps of the left foot for extra measure.

My answer to such assertions against self-promotion is, quite simply, capital B — friggn' — S! And I'll tell you why. One of the most emotional realities I've had to come to terms with is that if I want people to discover and read my work, then it's up to me to find ways to make sure they hear about it.

I found out the hard way that if you're not going to promote your work, then you might as well not even write it for public consumption. I mean, if you write a book you intend for others to read it. Right?

I'd say that's usually the way it works, unless, of course, we are trying to save our feelings from being hurt, and in that case we're likely to say something like we're just writing for ourselves. How's anyone going to manage to read your book if you keep it under wraps because you're too embarrassed or ashamed to self-promote it?

Self-promotion is necessary. Your work matters. And the world deserves to hear about it.

Ignore the naysayers, the haters and the holier-than-thou'ers who would never promote their own work (or anyone else's for that matter). I say it's more likely because they would never actually create anything worth promoting in the first place.

Self-promotion is not evil. With that said, I do agree that there are right ways and wrong ways to promote your writing, but I'm not here to debate who is doing it the right or wrong way.

I'm here to tell you it's got to be done and to give you a few tips on how to do it without being a jerk about it. Otherwise you're only writing for yourself, and in that case, a private little (secret) pocket notebook will do you just fine.

And let's be honest, you're work is worth it. So, please, whatever you do, don't hide it. But at the same time, don't bother publishing your work if you're not going to promote it.

Self-promotion is only a bad idea if your work sucks. In that case, if your work really isn't all that good, you'll find out soon enough because no one will help you spread the word about it no matter how much you promote it. And that's okay. At least you'll know what doesn't connect, and you can go back to the drawing board and create something better.

But I'll tell you what — if you're work is great (which I'm sure it is), because it teaches something, helps others, touches them in some way, or simply tells a fantastic story, then readers will appreciate that you took the time to promote your work so they could discover it.

How Cars Took Over the World

Did you know that Henry Ford created a full-scale motion picture department for the Ford Motor Company and that the department itself rivaled all of Hollywood's studios at the time in 1914?

The first movie produced by Mr. Ford's movie department (Highland Park) was "How Henry Ford Makes One Thousand Cars a Day."

Does that sound self-promotional to you? Perhaps it was, or perhaps it was simply "educational," but no one can argue with the fact that cars took over the world and Henry Ford changed forever how products were produced en masse.

He also changed how products were marketed. Ford's success with automobiles was in no small part thanks to the promotional movies he made. In the years between 1914 and 1920 Henry Ford's films were shown in over 4,000 theaters to five million people—roughly one-seventh of the nation's weekly movie-going audience. Such short promotional films would come to be known as commercials.

Let's Go Viral

We're so fascinated when we hear about a blog post or a video or a picture that went viral without any apparent attempts at self-promotion by the creator. Yes, it happens. And it's wonderful when it does, but I dare anyone to spend years writing, finally publish your work, and then merely sitting around waiting to get lucky enough for your work to take off on its own. It may happen, but the odds are not in your favor.

When most of us think of going viral, we tend to think of cute pets doing crazy things on YouTube videos and the views skyrocketing, but wait, not so fast… According to research testing by Chris Wilson over at Slate.com, a YouTube video's chance of going viral is, well, I'll quote him: "You might have better odds playing the lottery than of becoming a viral video sensation."

But guess what? The chances of going viral significantly improve when content is promoted.

Yep. You're going to have to promote your work. There's no way around it, if you want people to hear about it, you're going to have to delve into some good old-fashioned self-promotion. So put aside all of the BS you've heard about not promoting your own work and get ready to roll up your sleeves.

9 Ways to Promote Your Work without Being a Jerk:

1. Make sure it's your best work.

In other words, never publish a book (or anything) before it's ready. If your work is outstanding, then ship it. Great work is believed to promote itself, and the reality is that people will help spread the word about your work because it's awesome and they loved it.

2. Create an online platform.

Preferably a blog. A blog is a living, breathing presence online that is constantly updated. While you update your blog you also increase your readership. As you increase your readership, you build an audience to share your work with. If your audience deems your work worthy (awesome), they will help you spread the word. (See #1.)

3. Give them a good reason.

Why is your product, service, book, or whatever you're promoting, important to them? You need to have 'em at hello by making it clear what's in it for them.

Take my book, "Writer's Doubt" for example. It provides practical, workable strategies for any writer who is dealing with doubt. And what writer isn't dealing with doubt at some point in his or her writing career? The writers who want to do something about self-doubt will read it, but only if they are ready to do something about it. And why do we need such a book? Because self-doubt is the #1 enemy of writing! You're not immune. And that's okay, none of us are. But you can do something about it.

4. Be generous.

Help promote others regardless of whether they will return the favor or not. Promote others when they don't even know you're doing it. It's karma. And it's the right thing to do. Whose work have you promoted lately? A simple tweet will do, or share something on Facebook, or hey, just tell a good friend about a great book you recently read.

5. Give your work away for free.

Seth Godin did it with his book, *Unleashing the Ideavirus,* and it became the most downloaded eBook in history. How many people do you think Seth reached by giving away his book? Millions.

Free is a great way to spread your name for, well, free. Be sure to include your website address inside the content so readers can find you.

6. Connect and network with your "competition."

Competition isn't the same as it was years ago before the internet. Today the quickest and surest way to promote your work is to forge alliances with those you may have once considered competitors. You could be surprised to find out that when you help promote your "competition" they will promote you, too.

But here's the thing: you should promote other peoples work even if they don't promote yours. It makes you look good, and by gosh, it feels good, too! One word: Karma.

7. Get in on the buzz.

Weird Al Yankovic recently released a new album parodying several best-selling songs. He could have just as easily parodied unknown songs, but that wouldn't have been as much fun, and he would not have connected as quickly and easily with the buying public.

When Yankovic parodied Robin Thicke's hit song "Blurred Lines," *TIME* ran a piece on it and posted the video on their website. I don't think *TIME* would have done that for an unknown song by an unknown artist, do you? How's that for publicity?

Of course, we're talking about *THE* Weird Al Yankovic, not everyone has his pull, but then neither did Weird Al when he was just starting out. He's become a master at self-promotion by latching onto what's already hot, but still putting his own unique spin on it.

8. Be yourself. Be genuine.

Too often, people try to portray themselves as something they are not, and that only leads to frustration and anger. It's hard work to keep up appearances. So be honest about who you are to begin with, and you'll attract an audience based on the truth of who you are and what you are about. You don't need to be like John Smith or Jane Doe, so stop comparing yourself to them. You just need to be you.

9. Simply ask.

If you've created something awesome and you've used all of the previous tips, then the odds are you've put yourself in a good position to ask others to help you spread the word. So ask them.

The Next Step

We need your words. We need your voice. So please, by all means, tell us about your work. Share it with us. Don't hide it—no, don't do that!

Climbing Out of the Pit

By Bryan Hutchinson (Originally published on *Helping Writers Become Authors*)

Sometimes I want to give up. Sometimes I don't want to write anymore. And sometimes I do give up and stop writing. Have you been there? Stuck and filled with doubt.

Seth Godin has a great term called *"The Dip"* for when you're in a temporary setback, when you're ready to give up and decide to either quit or stick. But there's another dip, which is more about internal self-doubt, which I like to call "the pit." For many of us, it is a very real place we fall into when we feel "lesser-than," confused and exhausted from doubt, to the point of giving up.

The pit is deep, dark, cold, and damp. It's not a place I want to be, and yet, I've found myself there more often than I would like. It's good that it's not a nice place to be, because if it was pleasant, I might not climb back out. Maybe you wouldn't either.

Wanting to give up hurts because you know deep down that you want to continue, to strive and do your best. But for whatever reason, something is making you doubt yourself, and if you are not prepared, you can feel defeated. For me, this happens for different reasons at different times. To a degree, it is predictable, but still not easy to climb out of.

I grew up with an undiagnosed learning disorder and dyslexia, so I'm used to being the underdog. For the longest time, I didn't feel I was good enough.

But despite my limitations, somewhere deep inside myself I knew I wanted to be a writer. When I write, I feel good. It is when I am at peace and feel I am worth more than any diagnosis. I don't know why writing makes me feel so good, but it does, and I am grateful for that.

And yet, at the same time, writing can also be so very difficult. At times, sharing my writing leads to hearing things I don't want to hear, criticisms that can be harsh and even feel mean. But I write anyway.

For years, I hid my writing from the world because I believed I could not measure up. What could I say that would matter? Who would listen? In my twenties, I went through a major depression lasting almost a decade. Eventually, I found help through a wise, caring therapist. He helped me realize I was worth more than what the educational system and teachers said I was. I found ways to learn on my own, and since I never ran out of words, I discovered I had something of value to offer.

I believed I was "lesser-than" for so many years, hiding my writing and other talents to protect myself from living through ridicule and defeat. What finally helped me break free from my depression was writing my memoir, *One Boy's Struggle*. It was a therapeutic exercise my therapist suggested.

Initially, I had no intention of publishing it or sharing it with anyone. When I finally finished writing my story, I felt a great sense of relief. While writing had always been therapeutic for me, the difference was the details I wrote about my life. In writing the ugly, the bad and the good, too, I discovered I am a remarkable individual who found ways to make his way in the world despite disadvantages. We all have disadvantages. All of us.

Yes, I had to do things differently and learn most things on my own. But when you have a burning desire to do something, nothing and no one will be able to stop you.

You are remarkable. If you have a burning desire to be a writer, be a writer and don't worry about what someone might say about your writing. Sift. Take what's positive from what people say. Learn from it and leave everything else. Don't take it personally. Just keep writing.

Sometimes I forget my own advice when I feel overwhelmed, back in the bottom of the pit. Then I remind myself how far I have come, and how much I have worked to get to where I am. I use writing to tell my story, to help me climb the damp walls back into the light. Hopefully it will inspire others to do the same.

So whenever you find yourself filled with doubt and you feel like giving up, remember what you have done to get to where you are, the many challenges you've overcome. Think about all your achievements. And remember you are a unique, remarkable individual. Write anyway.

You can do it. You're a writer.

How to Embrace Your Fears to Create Your Best Work

By Bryan Hutchinson

Are you ready to answer the question? It's a simple one. It's the question that will reveal once and for all whether you're an artist or not.

Are you afraid?

Have you ever wished you could push the fear away? Or just get over it?

Don't wish such a thing, because neither you, nor anyone else, will ever be entirely fearless. And honestly, you shouldn't want to be. Fear is not your enemy.

The biggest problem with fear today is not fear itself. No, it is the belief that we should never be afraid, that we should be courageous and confident beyond measure. However, courage and confidence are not the result of an absence of fear. On the contrary, courage, confidence and even so-called, fearlessness are the results of facing, embracing, and finally, dancing with your fears. Dancing with your fears requires looking 'em in the eyes, raising your pen above the page, and writing.

It's okay to be afraid.

If you're not at least a little afraid, then that indicates you don't care enough about failing, about connecting, and about creating work that matters.

Too often, we look at prolific artists and wish we could be more like them because they seem to have nothing to fear. But that's not true. The most successful people, in this case those who consistently finish and ship, are the ones with the most to fear. They put themselves out there so many times that failure is not just a possibility, it is imminent.

Not everything everyone creates succeeds in the marketplace. Not every song Michael Jackson or Elvis Presley released into the world was a #1 hit. But that never stopped them from creating more.

So, yes, the odds of failure get higher with every piece of work that you ship.

Scary, isn't it? Good. It should be. Embrace fear because it means you're taking chances and creating when others are stalling and giving up. Fear has a natural way of weeding out those who don't care enough. So how much do you care?

You. Care. A. Lot.

You want to care so much that the mere thought of not creating scares you more than anything else. With that kind of fear, you'll create no matter what the results might be, and you'll pay more attention to what truly matters to you.

When embraced, fear can help us focus, stay the course, and create with passion. It's when you don't feel any fear that you should truly be worried, because that means your heart just isn't in it.

We love art not just because it's beautiful and rare, but also because we know the artist had to dance a glorious dance with fear to create such a masterpiece.

Our fear gives us our edge. Fear is an essential piece of the indescribable X-factor all memorable artists have in their work. Without fear, we would not need to go places that we'd rather not. Without fear, we would not try harder, worker longer, or attempt more than we've ever attempted before.

How we respond and live with our fear helps develop our personal signature. Your art, how it will be viewed and remembered, depends greatly on how you faced your fears. If you let fear control you and cause you to be insecure, overly frustrated, and doubt yourself, then your work will likely come across as weak, directionless, and incomplete.

If that's happened to you, it's okay. I know how you feel. I've been there, too. And the good news is that every day you have the opportunity to begin anew, to dance a new dance.

When you finally embrace fear and dance the glorious dance, your work will be considered bold and charming, beautiful and dignified, and even, unique, exquisite, and delicious...

We need fear.

Stop trying to avoid it, push it away, and feel comfortable. That won't work. Sometimes you need to be uncomfortable, dissatisfied and determined to break through the status quo and rock it!

You're going to have to face your fears. And be thankful for them.

We admire artists not just for the work they created, but because they remind us that great work comes from mastering not only the brush, the pen, or the lens, but rather, the fear within.

Master your fear by embracing, dancing and creating with it. You will never create work worthy of attention if you do not master fear.

Let's be clear here. I'm not talking about fear of a vicious wild animal, because by all means run like hell if you're in danger. No, you know the fear I've been talking about. The real fear that keeps you up at night. The fear you truly dread. The only way to brave *that* fear is to start creating with passion, to begin doing things that are risky, and to try doing things that might not work.

If you really want to remove fear, know that if/when you do (as if you could) you'll also be giving up the same power that drives you to create. Creative inclination and fear go hand in hand. You can't have one without the other. Just remember, when fear causes you sleepless nights and you're tossing and turning and wishing it would just go away—fear is not your enemy.

Fear is the fuel to your creative fire.

So what should we do?

Instead of tossing and turning and begging for sleep, get up, take action, and create something awesome! If you do that which you fear, you won't merely overcome it—no, you'll do something much better—you'll realize you're an artist.

And that's what artists do.

Face Fear the Wright Way and Write Your Best Work

By Bryan Hutchinson

It's dreadful. It's suffocating. It's absolutely, completely and utterly, debilitating. Yes. Yes, it can be. It can be all of those things. So how do you beat the fear that's holding you back?

I've been asked so many times how I overcame my fears. The truth is, though, I haven't. I live with fear every day. The difference between now and before is that I no longer let my fears eat me alive and control me, and I certainly don't allow them to stop me from creating work I care about. How? It's probably not the answer you're looking for. But then, that's why we rarely ever find it.

You will always be afraid. And sometimes, sometimes, you'll be very afraid. And that's okay. It means you're alive. You're human. You're an artist. You're audacious like that. You're a writer, dammit.

It means you create work you care about, and your work matters!

People who are creative live in perpetual fear. We fear no one will care, we fear looking stupid and we fear not living up to someone else's expectations. We fear haters and we fear praise. (What's too much and what's too little?)

The difference between writers who actually create work and those who don't is a very fine line between giving in to one's fear and creating anyway, being willing to look like a fool, to create imperfect work, and quite frankly, to be an artist.

We're all afraid. Every day. Being afraid is normal. At least, if you're human it is.

It's okay to be afraid. In fact, it's required. No one's ever created anything worthwhile they didn't fear wouldn't work. Once we understand that and accept it, we can only then finally live with our fears and create our best work. I'd love to describe what it feels like to not be afraid, but if I'm honest, I've never felt that way.

Fear isn't your enemy. Paralysis is. And paralysis is caused by doubt.

Now that, my fellow writers, is something to be afraid of. However, the good news is that there's a very effective (but not always simple) cure against paralysis for writers. It's called, writing.

If you have difficulty getting yourself to start writing (and who doesn't?), try visualizing yourself tip-tapping away at your keyboard, whizzing along in the flow. Visualize the end result. See yourself in a major bookstore with stacks of your books on a table ready for eager readers to scoop up and have signed by you.

Fly!

We enjoy flying today thanks to the determination of the Wright Brothers, but did you know they visualized flying even after failure upon failure? Their fears of failure and crashing, which all too often came true, couldn't stop them.

In Geneviève Behrend's book, *Your Invisible Power and How to Use It*, published in 1921, she writes that one of the Wright brothers would tell the other (after yet another failure), "It's all right, brother, I can see myself riding in that machine, and it travels easily and steadily."

See yourself writing, because after all, let's be honest, you know you really and truly are a writer. You will crash and burn (we all do), and if you submit your work for publication you will get rejected, and you will also eventually publish work that no one seems to care about except you.

And you know what? That's okay.

The Wright brothers were ridiculed and laughed at, and people told them they were absolutely nuts, and yet they did what everyone said could not be done.

You will succeed, too, but you will have your share of setbacks, and at times your fears will seem overwhelming and doubt will cause you to freeze and give up. When that happens, remember what one Wright brother told the other:

"It's all right, brother, I can see myself riding in that machine, and it travels easily and steadily."

Whenever you feel the fear and are doubtful, read the Wright brothers quote again (consider printing and framing it), and visualize stacks of your published books your readers are eagerly waiting for you to sign.

Now go. Write easily and steadily.

How to Edit Your Book until it is Finished

By Joe Bunting of *The Writer Practice*

Lately, I've been getting a lot of questions about how to edit a book. "I have a 60,000 word manuscript," people tell me, "but I don't know how to know if it's ready to publish."

Some of these writers want to finish up the manuscripts they began during NaNoWriMo. Others are in the middle of their first draft and are enthusiastically thinking ahead to their next steps.

However, they're all asking the same question: How do you know when your book is finished?

Writing Is Revision

Once you finish that last page, you will probably experience more pride than you ever have in your entire life, second only to giving birth. Go ahead and soak it up. Throw yourself a party. Take a few days off to celebrate.

Don't read your draft though, because as soon as you do, the awful reality of just how bad your book is will almost certainly dampen your mood. I love this quote from Michael Crichton:

"Books aren't written—they're rewritten. Including your own. It is one of the hardest things to accept, especially after the seventh rewrite hasn't quite done it."

Your book isn't finished until you revise it from beginning to end at least once (and almost always more than once). I could share a hundred quotes from celebrated writers that sound exactly like the one above, but instead, just trust me. When you finish your first draft, you have so much more work to do.

How the Editing Process Works

While the editing process looks different for every writer, a few things seem to work well for everyone. The best book I've ever read about the revision process is Stephen Koch's Writer's Workshop. If you want to learn more about this subject, I highly recommend picking up a copy.

Here are four suggestions on how to edit your book:

1. Read Your Book

After you finish your first draft, read your manuscript once by yourself. Don't edit. Don't cross out anything. The purpose of this step is not to revise but to get a fresh perspective on the book and see what holes need filling.

While I wouldn't suggest doing any heavy duty editing, you're welcome to take notes or jot down any ideas you have for the next step.

2. Write 10 Scenarios

This trick is especially great for fiction writers.

In my college art class, our first assignment was to draw a quick sketch of a tea cup 100 times. Yes, I was very familiar with that tea cup by the end of the assignment. The hard part was that each drawing had to be different. After I drew the teacup from a few normal perspectives, I was forced to get creative. I started drawing levitating tea cups, tea cups that were sawn in half, cubist tea cups, and even tea cup wallpaper.

Scenarios function the same way. They're quick summaries of your entire book in just a few thousand words. By telling a summarized version of your story ten different ways, you get new ideas about your book's core essentials, who the main important characters are, which ideas are most central, and how to structure your book in the most interesting way possible.

Scenarios shouldn't take longer than a day to write, and can be as short as 2,000 to 3,000 words for a book and 300 to 500 words for a short story. The key is to have fun and be creative!

3. Three Drafts

While most professional writers write three drafts or more, there are quite a few single-drafters out there. However, single-drafters usually spend much longer on their first drafts than most writers, so that by the end, they probably rewrite more than multi-drafters.

After your first draft, your second draft is meant for major structural fixes. If you found any major holes in the reading stage, your second draft is a great time to write or rewrite chapters and scenes. After the discoveries you make in your scenarios, you may even decide to rewrite the whole book from the beginning.

I wouldn't do much polishing until your third draft. That would be like sanding down the foundation of your house. Your final touches don't come until your third draft. First drafts are for digging the book's foundation, second drafts for framing the house, and third drafts for finish work.

4. Send It to Friends

How do you know when your book is finished? Leonard da Vinci once said, "Art is never finished, only abandoned." However, there is a trick to knowing when to "abandon" your book and send it out into the world.

Whenever I finish any draft except for the first—which is for my eyes only—I send my manuscript to a group of up to 30 friends to give me feedback. Through these beta readers I'm able to get a sense of what my book really is, not what I think it is. When you edit your book, you get too close to the work to have any rational perspective. Beta readers bring fresh eyes, and by listening to them as they talk about your book, you'll be able to see whether it's ready for the world.

When to Hire an Editor

Self-published books have a bad rap for poor editing. However, this isn't completely fair. If you buy a first printing of a traditionally published book, you will likely find two or three typos. By the time the publisher is in their second printing, these have all been fixed. Most people just don't read first printings.

Typos happen. You can have a team of 20 people looking for errors in your book and still, when it's finally published, your second cousin will call you to tell you there's a typo on page 276.

That being said, if you want to self-publish, please hire a professional editor. Not only will you have a better book because of it, good editing is the best way to learn the writing craft.

If you can afford it, I recommend hiring an editor to critique your book after your second draft, giving a high-level overview of your major problems. After your third draft, it's essential that you hire a line editor or copy editor to go through your prose with a fine-tooth comb.

Give yourself the gift of the best book you could have written. The authors I work with are always so much happier after editing than before. You'll be glad you invested in it.

6 Ways to Enjoy the Editing Process (Seriously!)

By Shanan Haislip

Writing's easy; editing's hard. Getting lost in the fun and the discovery of putting down words can make up for the times when the words don't come easily. But it's during the editing process that you're forced to look at the flaws in your creation.

How could that possibly be any fun? Here are a few ways you can inject a little fun into the drudgery of the editing process:

6. Err on the Side of Outrageous

Easy metaphors, comfortable sentence structures, and familiar details are solid and predictable, but now that your first draft is finished, you've got to weed out the unnecessarily ordinary. (Any "rushing river" or "windswept beach" similes sneak in? Take 'em out) Consider some more outrageous and outlandish—and ultimately, more memorable—constructs.

Need inspiration? My go-to when I want to get in the mood to take some risks is actually an English undergrad staple: T.S. Eliot's "The Love Song of J. Alfred Prufrock." This poem is unusually expressive, almost to a fault. Take these lines:

Let us go then, you and I,

When the evening is spread out against the sky

Like a patient etherized upon a table;

Can you go bolder than comparing an evening sky to someone who's been anesthetized on a hospital gurney?

5. Try Some Ridiculous Constraints for Fresh Perspective

"Lipogram" is just a fancy name for the games writers play when they're on the editing track and running out of steam. One of the most famous is the novel Gadsby, penned by Ernest Vincent Wright and written entirely without using the letter "E."

Another editing technique, called E-Prime, involves eliminating all forms of the verb "to be" from your writing. No ams, is-es, was-es, weres, bes, beings, and beens, no passive voice, no unclear connections between subjects and objects.

Consider adopting one of these constraints or just make one up! It can be exasperating, but also fun.

4. Remember Blaise Pascal's Words

One of the reasons editing can be difficult is the sheer amount of time it takes, sometimes even longer than writing the first draft. And that's okay! If your time commitment to editing is getting you down, remember this humorous quote, attributed to 17th-century mathematician, physicist and philosopher Blaise Pascal:

"I have only made this letter longer because I have not had the time to make it shorter."

3. Engage Your Secret Weapon

Every writer needs a weapon in his or her arsenal to help thaw the creative flow, which tends to get frozen during editing. Do you have a favorite piece of writing you've done recently? Something that, when you re-read it, gives you an extra boost of confidence in your chosen profession? Make that your secret weapon during the editing process!

When you hit a rough patch, pull out your favorite piece of writing and re-read it as a small reminder of what you're capable of (and keep editing).

2. Sleep. A lot.

This probably sounds patronizingly simple, but it's really easy to think, "Just one more page," and sacrifice sleep to push through the daunting pile of manuscript pages. Whenever I do this, I wind up in an awful mood that tends to stick around until I've had a nap. Like a giant, caffeine-addled toddler.

Be mindful of a regular sleep schedule, and consider using a sleep tracker app to help you monitor your quality and quantity of shut-eye.

1. Simply Refuse to Worry

The worst part about editing isn't the heavy mental lifting, or even the sheer amount of time it requires. Instead, it's the worry that you're about to discover that the draft you're working on simply won't work. You're searching for your writing's fatal flaw.

Stress can make editing seem daunting and even a little scary, but remember that, without exception, those types of fears are totally unfounded. Even novels with fatal flaws can be resurrected during editing, and if you encounter incoherence, you can always delete the offending section and try again. No worries!

6 Quick Tricks to Help You Tighten Up Your Writing

By C.S. Lakin of *Live Write Thrive*

Writers often think about tightening their writing. Just what does that mean? And how is it done? Is there a way that writers can tighten up their writing without losing their voice or compromising their writing style?

Like sneaky calories, many unwanted words and phrases find their way into our writing unnoticed and bog it down. The goal should be to write in a concise fashion so that our meaning is clearly understood. It's not all that tricky to do. And don't worry—this can be done without adversely cramping a writer's style.

That's not to say these tips are a cure-all for major flaws in a story, article, or book. But similar to the get-in-shape-fast programs, here are some simple things writers can do to tighten sentences, shed unwanted words, and tone and shape the whole "body" of work.

1. Eliminate Fatty Words from Your "Diet"

Make a list of your weasel words. Those are the words you throw in out of habit. Often they are pesky adverbs like very and just. Or phrases like began to or started to. Grab a random page of your document and see if you can eliminate at least one or two words from every sentence. It may not be possible, but it's a good exercise. If the word doesn't add importance to a sentence, it should go. Then attack the rest of your novel.

2. Reword Passive Voice Where Possible

Whether referring to general passive ("The food was eaten by me" instead of "I ate the food") or present progressive passive ("The food is being served" instead of "the waiters served the food"), most of the time a sentence will be stronger if the passive voice is avoided. An easy way to seek and destroy unwanted passive construction is do a "Find" for ing, was, is, it was, and there was, to name a few.

3. Avoid Circumlocution

I just love that word, so I have to use it. Don't use two words when one will do. Don't use four when three will do. If two adjectives are similar, pick the best one and toss the other.

4. Ditch the Extraneous Speaker and Narrative Tags

If you are writing fiction or narrative nonfiction, you may have dialog in your piece. Be aware that if the reader knows who is speaking, you don't need to tell them over and over—especially in a scene with only two characters. And remove all those flowery verbs that stick out, such as quizzed, extrapolated, exclaimed, and interjected. Just use said and asked, and maybe an occasional replied or answered. Really. Less is more . . . effective.

5. Search and Destroy Repetition

We tend to repeat words, phrases, or ideas in the same paragraph. Sometimes that's a good thing to do, to drive home a point, perhaps in summary at the end of a section or subheading. But writers often try to say the same thing in a different way, and instead of adding new material they are essentially rehashing what they've already said. One great way to catch those repetitive words is to hear your piece read aloud using a software program like Natural Reader.

6. And a Word about Backstory . . .

Yes, the dreaded backstory, which novelists have been told to shun in the first chapters of a novel. But really, do you need it? Take a look at all the places you have backstory and boil down just a few lines of the most important information you feel the reader must know to "get" the story. Then see if you can have a character either think or say these things instead of going into lengthy narrative. Look for any passage that feels like author intrusion or an info dump and find another way to impart the information.

If you're the kind of writer that needs to "add weight" to your skimpy book, you have a different challenge, and the problem won't be solved by ignoring all the above tips. Remember, it's the unwanted fat you want to eliminate. Be sure what you add to a skimpy novel is muscle, not fat.

And for the rest of us who overwrite, be reassured that by implementing these easy tips, you can help trim those unwanted "pounds" from your pages and tighten up your writing.

How to Write Your Story in 6 Steps

By Claire DeBoer of *The Gift of Writing*

These days everyone's talking about writing your story. Not just any old story, but the story of your life, the road map that got you to where you are today. For most of us that's a pretty daunting thought. I mean, why would anyone be interested in hearing our story anyway?

Life-Changing

Well, I'm a big proponent of this personal story writing business, and I'll tell you why: it changed my life.

I used to write fiction. I loved hiding behind the facades of the characters I created. But then my work led me into writing for a magazine where people share their personal stories, and I found myself on unfamiliar territory.

I actually had no interest in sharing my story—I wasn't a fiction writer for nothing. I thought my past was empty and depressing. But given my role as both a writer and editor for this magazine, I really didn't have much choice.

Resistance

So I sat down at my computer and with absolute resistance I began to write the truth of my life. I was full of fear—afraid to reveal my authentic self and the vulnerability that came with doing it. I was also fearful that no one would give a hoot about my story.

My resistance to the process resulted in quite the crappy effort. Apparently my chief editor thought so, too. She sent the article back to me with these words: "go deeper." Not quite the response I was looking for.

So I went back to my computer, stared at a blank page for a while, and began to write. But this time I didn't write from a place of resistance, I wrote from the heart.

The result was tears, not just on my part, but my editor's, too.

But more important than the tears was the overwhelming sense of release. In reconnecting with my story, I somehow gave it a voice. I gave myself a voice that needed to be heard.

I have continued to write my story and to pursue the practice of helping others do the same. Not only do I believe that telling our stories is an important way to get to know ourselves and find healing, I also believe it's a way to connect with others on a deeply authentic level.

Where Do We Begin?

Writing our personal stories is the most vulnerable kind of writing we can do. We fear being laughed at, rejected, or that our words will be met with silence. And in turn, we ourselves remain silent.

Through the process I have found six important steps to be helpful:

1. Tap Into Your Emotions

Your story won't resonate with others if it is void of emotion, as I discovered when writing that first draft of my own story. So take out your paper and pen and write down some key feelings that you associate with your life so far. Then write something about each feeling and the story behind it.

2. List the Turning Points

People often make the mistake of starting with their earliest childhood memory and moving through their story chronologically. But rather than starting at the beginning, it's more helpful to make a list of your life's key turning points—those times when you were standing at a crossroads and the direction you chose marked a significant change in your life.

3. Write Everything Down

It might not seem like much at the time but it's amazing how one memory leads to another and allows you to go deeper into your story. As with all writing, you may not use many of the scenes you write, but that doesn't mean they don't have a purpose.

4. Use the Senses

The one thing that will help you explore long forgotten memories is to use your senses. As you recall events, try to remember the smells, tastes and sounds that accompany them. Not only will this help you remember details, it will also enrich your writing.

5. Find the Theme

Once you have compiled a large number of significant scenes, it's likely you will begin to see a theme emerging. Your theme is the central question driving your story. The ability to carry this theme through the sequence of events you have recorded is what will turn your individual scenes into one story. It may be that you discover more than one theme. That's okay; it's likely there will be one that stands apart from the others.

6. Tell a Story

You have your theme and a multitude of scenes; you've gone through a box of tissues in the process of exploring your emotions, but have you told a story? As you begin to work on pulling it all together, focus on the reader. The best stories are ultimately those that connect with the reader the most.

This process of telling your story is, I believe, one of the most rewarding and clarifying things you can do for yourself, and for others.

So step into that place of discomfort and write the words that will bring freedom and meaning to your life. Is it not time?

Why Writers Self-destruct and 5 Ways to Thrive Instead

By Bryan Hutchinson

In *The Color of Money*, the only movie for which Paul Newman ever won a Best Actor Oscar, there's a scene near the end where he's playing against the legendary real-life pool player Steve "The Miz" Mizerack. After Steve loses to Paul, Steve says, "I didn't deserve that." And without the slightest hesitation, Paul's character, Fast Eddie Felson, replies, "Yes, you did."

The reason Fast Eddie said, "Yes, you did," is the same reason too many writers the world over self-destruct, fail, and quit writing.

How to Be a Confident Writer

When I used to coach and teach pool-billiards the first thing I would teach is the "mental game." The mental game is where players win or lose regardless of how great their technical skills might be.

According to Dr. Jorge Valverde, the world-renowned sports psychologist and creator of the Valverde System, the percentage of the mental game is 80% to 90%.

In sports, it's quite easy to demonstrate how decisive the mental game is, especially in pool. In order to demonstrate to students the mental game in action, I would take them to pool tournaments to watch and, more importantly, listen to players before, during, and after matches.

Pool players are notorious for the way they vocally express themselves at tournaments. The difference between the winners and losers is glaring, in that those who go on to reach the higher brackets are typically the players who are speaking positive, can-do, winning words.

On the other hand, it is even easier to identify those who will not advance, because they are continuously vocalizing every reason under the sun why they are not playing well and why other players have advantages or, even worse, why "something" is holding them back from excelling. After losing matches, these are the players you tend to hear say, "I didn't deserve that."

Yes, they did. Because they self-destructed, mentally quit, and, in a negative state of mind, they squandered any and all opportunities to win. It's what Steve Mizerack characterized so well in *The Color of Money*: A losing mentality.

Seems pretty cut-and-dried, doesn't it? And you know what? It is.

Technical proficiency and talent are important, but are only worth 10% to 20% of the game. If a player wants to play her best and win, she must work on building her self-confidence, overcome her fears and doubts, and ultimately, she must cultivate an overall winning attitude. She doesn't have to be perfect, but she must accept that she has a chance to win every time she competes.

I'm not talking about being a jerk and stating you're the best thing since sliced bread. No. That's grandiose BS. And doesn't work. Norman Vincent Peale said it best in one of my all-time favorite quotes:

"Without a humble but reasonable confidence in your own powers you cannot be successful or happy."

Cultivating a confident, honest, yet humble, winning attitude takes work. In fact, I'd go so far as to say that working on one's attitude is the main reason to compete, because it forces you to look within and improve. Just as writing does. Writers must work on their mental game, too.

You don't need to play sports in order to work on the "mental game," and you don't need another person to compete. As a writer, your competitor is yourself – who you were yesterday, who you are today, and who you will be tomorrow.

The goal should be to improve every day as a writer and as a person.

Just as pool players are notorious for the way they express themselves at tournaments, writers are notorious for being stuck in doubt, beaten by their own inner negative self-talk, and unable to write anything they consider worth diddly – friggn' – squat. (I've been there.)

But you know what? It comes with the territory and is absolutely normal. Even so, as normal as it may be, negative self-talk is not helpful and only serves to set you up to give up and quit, or create work you're not proud of.

For those of us chastising ourselves incessantly, all the while muttering the dreadful words, "I don't deserve this," Fast Eddie Felson would have blunt words. "Yes, you do." It's the reason writers the world over self-destruct, fail, and quit. Ashes to ashes. Dust to dust.

A scene from *The Color of Money* burned into my memory is the look on Steve Mizerak's face after Paul Newman said those honest, revealing words. No wonder the movie was nominated for an Academy Award for best writing. The story was not as much about pool as it was about human nature.

"Pool excellence is *not* about excellent pool." –Eddie Felson

The same could be said of writing.

5 Tips on How to Thrive as a Writer

What if writing isn't all that different from sports? For example, the technical aspects (punctuation, grammar, and syntax, etc…) get most of the attention, but it's the mental game that matters most. After all, if you doubt your ability to write a novel, or to write a good novel, or to write a novel others will want to read (see, this can go on all day), it doesn't matter how technically proficient you are at writing. You must be able to trust your ability to write words that matter.

1. Become mindful of what you say to yourself about yourself

Writing is, for the most part, a solitary job, and it's easy to get caught up and overwhelmed by negative thoughts without even realizing it until it is too late. When the negative, self-critical voice comes, be aware of it and immediately tell it to be quiet, because you're busy writing. And continue writing. It's a simple technique that works.

2. Make a list of your accomplishments

The negative voice in your head is a master at making you aware of your failures, both the real and the imagined, and if you're not careful it's easy to fall into the trap of believing you've never accomplished anything.

When the self-sabotaging voice tries to convince you that you are worthless and couldn't write an opening paragraph to save your life, read your list of accomplishments, and then say aloud with conviction, "I am well able. I am a writer."

3. Make a list of positive affirmations

I used to underestimate the power of positive affirmations because I thought they were silly. I eventually learned the reason this is such a popular suggestion. Positive affirmations work.

Make a list of affirmations you believe in, write a few of the most powerful on little pieces of paper, and put them in places you will constantly see them. And when you see them, say them aloud.

4. Stop complaining

We all do it. Most of the time we don't even realize it. Examples are, "My draft is crap. No. It's worse. Calling it crap is too good for it." – "I can't come up with any ideas. I'm an idiot. Other people come up with great ideas easily." – "I just wasted another day staring at the screen writing nothing but gibberish. I'm worthless. I'm nothing. And I'm ugly, too!"

Okay folks, calm down. The end of the world isn't upon us and you're a lot better looking than you think you are, and you're a much better writer than you think you are.

5. Be YOU!

You are uniquely you. Embrace yourself as you are. Stop comparing yourself to others. When we compare ourselves to others we come up short 99% of the time.

You Are Enough

You're better than you think you are. You have it in you to write a masterpiece. And when you finish your first masterpiece, you'll write another and then another. It doesn't matter how much you've already written, your best is still to come. But if you're stuck in Writer's Doubt and allow the harshest critic of all, your own internal negative voice, to kill your enthusiasm – you'll never write the words that deserve to be written by you.

Repeat after me: "I write stories that matter."

Yes, you do.

The 3 Essentials that Determine Your Writing Success

By Marcy McKay

Let's face it, questions constantly haunt us about our writing: Is my work any good? - Will others like it? - Will I find a literary agent or editor?

There are so many outcomes beyond our control, but all that stinkin'-thinkin' leads to...

Self-Doubt

In order to succeed, writing requires your mind, body and spirit. If you're struggling to create, that may be your problem. You might be using only 1/3 of yourself to write and it could be killing your craft.

Maybe you should give another area more attention to become a whole writer and more successful. Let's explore each of these a little closer.

1 . Mind

This tends to the inner part of ourselves. Try these suggestions to help your mind improve your writing:

- Write – You'd think this is obvious, but I know countless people who want to write, talk about it, but don't do the work. It's simple. Writing is a habit. It takes practice. The more you write, the better you become. Every day is best, but do what you can.

- Read – Writers write, but they also read. Fiction. Nonfiction. Read books in your genre, read for enjoyment, then if you really love the book, read it again as a student of the craft.
- Pay Attention to Your Thoughts – This isn't "woo-woo nonsense." It works. Our actions follow our thoughts. The next time you're having a bad day, I'll bet you're having negative thoughts. Negative thoughts = negative actions. Positive thoughts = positive actions. Think you can't be a New York Times Best-Selling Author? You're right, you can't. Think you can? Now, you have a shot...

2. Body

This tends to the outer part of ourselves. Try these suggestions to help your body improve your writing:

- Get Enough Sleep – I mean 8 hours of continuous sleep. I failed with this years ago. When my kids were little (ages three and a newborn), I'd go to sleep every night by 9 p.m. (that was easy, I was exhausted). I dragged myself out of bed every day by 3 a.m. and wrote until 6 or 7 a.m. when my kids woke up. I did that for years. Bad idea. I would've accomplished so much more if I'd slept two more hours and written from 5 to 6 or 7 a.m. Strive for a bare minimum of 6 consecutive hours of sleep.
- Eat Junk, Feel like Junk – If most of your meals come from to-go bags or cardboard boxes, then you're eating crap. Stay away from sugar, too. (Alcohol is sugar.) Eat fresh vegetables, fruits, and lean protein. Everything healthful you eat is brain fuel. Use it.
- Exercise – Calm down, you don't have to get a gym membership, but think of all those hours you log in front of a computer? Take breaks every hour or so. Get up and move around. Even better, take a walk outside or move your body in some way daily.

3. Spirit

This is our inner and outer parts combined and makes up the essence of YOU. Try these suggestions to help your spirit improve your writing:

- Unplug – Technology is great, but it also kills our creativity. Just like our cell phones need to recharge every day, so do our minds and bodies. At least once a week (more is even better), try to be "technology free" for at least five hours.
- Get Still – Everyday, be still for 10 minutes, doing nothing. You don't have to pretzel your legs together or chant "ohhhhmmm." Just sit or lie down somewhere comfortable. Your mind will wander. That's okay. Watch your thoughts like a movie. I do it in bed each morning when I wake up. It's a great way to start the day.
- Surround Yourself With Positive People – Life is hard: financial struggles, divorce, addiction and illness. Still, try to be around people who believe in you and your dream. If you can't get away from the nay-sayers, try to tune them out. Remember, you're above anyone trying to bring you down.

Bottom-line: Writers write.

We cannot control every outcome with our writing, but I've found when I actively focused on what I COULD control, my writing improved as well.

Are You Unwittingly Sabotaging Yourself by Talking About Your Writing?

By Ali Luke of *Aliventures*

You've got a great idea for a novel, and you can hardly stop yourself from telling your friends about it. The only problem is, the more you talk about your idea, the harder it seems to be to get started. Or … you're planning to start a blog, and you've been chatting to your partner about it for weeks. Whenever you sit down to draft a post, though, you find yourself staring at a blank screen.

What's going on?

"Talking" here also covers Facebook, forums, Twitter, and other non-verbal forms of chatter!

Talking Can Scratch that Writing Itch

All writers want – need – to share their thoughts with the world. They invent imaginary people, or come up with great new ideas, or work out cool plot twists. The problem is, if you spend too much time talking about your story or blog or other writing plans, you're likely to find that your writing energy dissipates. When you sit down to write, you might feel like you no longer need to. You've already explored and expressed those ideas.

Talking about writing can also make you feel like you've accomplished something. After all, if your friends all know you're going to write the Great American Novel any day now, you may feel like a writer already – even if you've not set a single word down on paper.

Other People May Discourage You

Instead of talking about the details of your work-in-progress, you discuss your writing more broadly — in terms of your career and major goals. Some of your friends roll their eyes. They think of writers as some special breed, and they don't believe that you can call yourself a writer. (Ignore them; you are a writer!)

Another says, "But you'll never make any money writing." A third friend adds, trying to be kind, "It's a lovely dream. But it's not very realistic, is it?"

At best, perhaps someone offers a wildly different alterative plan, telling you, "The real money is in romance novels," or "Why don't you write a children's book?" — however far this is from your dreams.

Your friends and family usually don't mean to make you feel down. They might be worried that you'll go for your dreams and fail, so they're trying to protect you. Or they might have no idea why you'd want to be a writer. Occasionally, they might feel threatened by your ambition — especially if they've given up on creative ideas of their own.

Talking about writing isn't always bad, though. Done right, it can be a great way to get inspired and motivated. Here's how:

Find Fellow Writers Who'll Support and Encourage You

Other writers understand what it's like — the good and the bad. Unlike non-writing friends, they'll get it. They'll help you celebrate the successes that other friends might not understand, and they'll encourage you to keep going when things are tough.

They know you don't want to switch genres just because there might be more money in it. They know that it's not really about the money. They know what you mean when you talk about a character "coming to life." They can encourage you to take a step outside your comfort zone.

Some writers find it's helpful to get together and write at the same time, perhaps in a coffee shop, or one person's house. (If you live in a major city, you may well find organized events for this – particularly during November for National Novel Writing Month.)

Get Friends to Keep You Accountable

Non-writing friends can still help – as can your blog readers, Twitter followers, fellow forum members, and other online acquaintances. You might not want to share in-depth details about your fight against plot holes, or your struggles to keep your characters in line ... but you could tell them your word count goal for the week ahead.

Being accountable (and having a deadline) is incredibly helpful. If all your Facebook friends know that you're aiming to write 2,000 words before midnight on Sunday, you'll be more motivated to keep on writing.

Talk Through a Problem with a Writing Buddy

Sometimes, you're not stalled because of any lack of motivation. You've got the time and energy to write – but something's not working. Maybe you need a character to act in a certain way to meet the demands of the plot – but you can't quite make their behavior fit.

Maybe you're debating between several different directions for your story. Maybe you need a back-story for your protagonist – but you don't know what. This is where a writing buddy can help. Ideally, this will be someone at a similar level of writing to you. (If they're a total newbie and you've had three novels published, or vice versa, it's not going to work.)

Talk through the problem. Explain where you've got to, and what's not working. Sometimes, simply talking it out can help you see a solution. Other times, your buddy might make suggestions that help. (Even if your response is "no, that would never work," you might at least rule out a particular idea!)

Why You Need to Do Something Stupid (to Succeed as a Writer)

By Bryan Hutchinson

Too many of us stop before we get started. So we tend to believe it's the starting that is the hardest part of, well, getting started. But it's not. Not by a long shot.

There's something else that holds you back from giving us your best work. Something devastating. And at one point or another, we all must figure out how to overcome it or live the rest of our lives in mediocrity, obscurity, and even regret.

If you never start we'll never get to read, view, or listen to you, and that would be a shame. So what can you do about it?

Do. Something. Stupid.

If you think about it a while, I know you'll realize the truth. It's not other people who hold you back, and although it might seem like it at times, it's not your "circumstances," either.

The real culprit, what is, in fact, holding you back from creating your best work, is:

Y.O.U.

How? It's those secret thoughts of yours that are doing it. The ones you don't like to admit exist. They are the self-deprecating thoughts that are so ingrained in your psyche that no matter how you rationalize to yourself that they are unjustified, you invariably succumb to the belief that they are true.

"I was stupid to think I could do it. And even if I did it, 'they' would think it's stupid. Yep. It was a stupid idea anyway."

Then I discovered the secret that set me free:

Anything worth doing always seems stupid at first.

Let's not allow our negative self-talk to sabotage our art and our chances at success. The real problem when we talk ourselves out of starting is that we put our ideas and ourselves down in order to avoid looking and feeling foolish.

We're not always afraid of failure itself. We're more afraid of the repercussions of failing and being considered an idiot for thinking we could get away with it. You really thought you could create something that matters? Don't be stupid. Think again. Stop this foolishness. Be normal. Be average. Fit in.

We all think such thoughts. No matter how well we keep them hidden, they are there, taunting and ridiculing us.

Don't be stupid. You idiot!

So how do you overcome this unyielding tension between creating something meaningful and believing that it's stupid? In order to do something worthwhile, you must become willing to go ahead and create anyway. You must ignore the idea that you need to be, and that others need to see you as, perfect.

And frankly, my friend, the reality is we're not perfect. So let's stop trying to be.

To create something that matters, you've got to be willing to suffer the discomfort of criticism, biases, and outright unfairness. But you also must be willing to accept praise, joy, and success.

It's okay to do something that seems stupid, as long as you do it. Someone's got to. It might as well be you.

A stupid idea about a book for writers:

I've never passed an English class in my life, I was kicked out of high school, and I was told by one of my English professors in college that I'd never be a writer. So writing a book about writing, well, that was a pretty stupid idea. Don't you think? But I did it. The book (as you may already know) is titled *Writer's Doubt* and it currently has over 50 five-star reviews on Amazon. It's helping writers do what they love to do—write.

Even a king, and a stupid idea about giving speeches:

King George VI of England had a crippling stammer and was absolutely terrified by the idea of speaking in public. He didn't just believe he would sound stupid if he must address his nation, he knew it for a verifiable fact.

And yet, with the help of a gifted speech therapist, after 9 other speech experts had utterly failed, he not only overcame his speech impediment, his speeches during World War 2 are now credited for uniting Britain. (His story was recounted in the Academy Award winning movie, *The King's Speech*.)

Your stupidest idea could be your best idea, ever. Don't underestimate it.

So what's really stopping you?

How about taking a chance and doing something crazy? Go ahead and acknowledge that your idea might be a stupid one. And you know what? That's okay. Because anything worth doing doesn't need someone else's stamp of approval as a great idea. It just needs to be done to the best of your ability.

Go for it.

Why Failure IS an Option for Writers

By Kate Foley of *The Magic Violinist*

"Failure is not an option."

We hear it all the time. People have even made T-shirts with that motto. And by saying it's not an option, we associate failure as a negative thing.

But what if it were an option?

What holds us back when we're writing? What causes us to stop in the middle of a sentence and hit the backspace button? For me—and for many of you, I'm sure—there are three things:

1. *I'm stuck.*

2. *I'm bored.*

3. *I'm scared.*

Which one used to stop me the most? If you thought number three, you're right!

Early on in the stages of writing—before I found fantastic writing websites, like "The Write Practice" and "Positive Writer"—I would find myself stopping and deleting more often than I was click-clacking away on my keyboard.

It was infuriating, and I had no idea what was wrong. I knew exactly where my story was going, but I couldn't for the life of me find a way to get there. After a few minutes of digging, I found the problem. I was scared. Scared of upsetting my readers, scared of what people would think of me, scared of making a mistake. But what's the worst that could happen if I made a mistake?

The worst thing would be making that mistake, and mistakes can be fixed. When I'm editing, I constantly think, "Oh, there's where I went wrong. I'll be sure not to do that again." And I fix it.

"Failing" has made me a better writer.

If I hadn't made that mistake—or fifty, or hundreds of those mistakes—I wouldn't have learned from it. If you're not learning something about writing each day, you're not growing as a writer.

Stop making failure a negative thing and start writing. Don't be afraid to make mistakes and start creating. And if you do mess up, do your best to learn from it. Trust me; you'll be much better off.

What if your first book was sold to a publisher quickly, but then each of your next 5 books were turned down? That exact scenario happened to none other than Danielle Steel, currently the bestselling author alive and the fourth bestselling author of all time.

"I thought I should write a book! I tried and I did, and it sold remarkably quickly. Then I thought I'll do this again, but then I wrote five others that nobody ever wanted. I had five unpublished in between my first and the next published book." —Danielle Steel

Keep learning. Keep writing. Keep growing.

4 Effective Ways to Beat Burnout

By Shanan Haislip

It goes beyond mere writer's block. It doesn't care about deadlines and can stopper your writing voice for months at a time. It's deep, it's baffling and it's not often talked about in writing circles.

It's writer's burnout.

And whether you're published or not, prolific or not, writer's burnout is coming for you. In fact, I'm sure you've already experienced it, and perhaps you're even battling it right now. Are you ready to beat it?

What's Writer's Burnout?

Unlike writer's block, in which your writing voice gets tangled in a web of competing thoughts and objectives, writer's burnout carries a tinge of resignation. You're not just temporarily silenced, you're sick of the entire process of getting your voice unstuck.

Not caring as deeply as you did just moments ago can be a profoundly disconcerting experience, and as a result, not many writers talk about how burnout saps your will to do creative work.

Ultimately, you just get tired of writing. You're suddenly, totally over this whole writing business. And because all your writer friends are chirping "#amwriting! Word count done for today!" on Twitter and in your writing groups, you wonder if something's actually wrong with you.

Don't worry; nothing's wrong with you.

But writer's burnout won't go away on its own. Here are four strategies to help clear it out and get you back to the business at hand.

Beating Writer's Burnout

4. Re-route your creative energy

Even on the best of days, writing can be a slog. If you've exhausted your mental resources and no longer have the "fight" left in you, give yourself permission to walk away. Without guilt, without nervously wondering when you'll next get butt-in-chair time.

Pull your creativity in a different direction. Rearrange a bookshelf. Stop by a local library and check out the local art and historical exhibits it houses. Borrow a CD by an artist you've never heard of. Sit in a chair and listen to it.

3. Deliberately leave the writing, and reconnect with a loved one

The spouses and family members of writers are in a privileged and often thankless position. Think about it. They tolerate those moments when you simply vanish inside your own mind, working out plot points or connecting dots no one else can see. They have to get used to you writing in their vicinity, seemingly so available yet so completely far away.

Go back to them. Concentrate all your energy on making sure they know how much they matter to you, how interested you really are in their lives, and just relax in their company for some time. You'll recharge more than just your creative batteries.

2. Give your busy mind a vacation

A truth universally acknowledged of writers and other creative people: Our minds are very busy. Annoyingly busy. We can't shut them off. They're always running, talking, connecting, deconstructing, rebuilding, wondering, and worrying.

However, it's also truth that where the body goes, the mind follows. For a few days or weeks, throw yourself into your day job (if you have one). Lose yourself in physical activity (and no, it doesn't have to be exercise, though that helps). Clean out a gutter. Split some wood. Walk one station farther down the subway line before you hop onboard. Fix your old mountain bike and take it for a spin.

Extra credit: If you don't have children of your own, offer to babysit your cousins, nieces, nephews, or close friends' kids for a few hours. Being around kids has a way of re-routing your stuck thought processes. They also wear you out, which can be a good thing.

1. Permit yourself to be sick of writing for a while

Writers don't like to talk about when they're sick of words and writing and their characters. They isolate themselves, freezing their frustration in time. With no way to let their feelings out, the writer's burnout doesn't run its course.

When you're feeling a bout of burnout coming on, try strategies 2-4, but remember that you'll get over it faster if you're open about feeling more #notwriting than #amwriting. (And I bet you'll find some voices out their willing to commiserate. Misery loves company.)

And before you know it, your burnout will fade. You will want to start writing again. It'll take some time, but the words will be back. I promise!

Do not Let the *Play-It-Safers* Talk You Out of Your Writing Potential

By Bryan Hutchinson (Originally published on *Bestseller Labs*)

No matter what your personal ambitions are as a writer, there will always be play-it-safers who tell you writing is a bad choice, it's not worth it, there's no money in it and, well, basically you need to lower your expectations and live down here with the rest of us.

So stop aiming so high, you're just going to hurt yourself or hurt someone else when you fail.

How many people face such discouragement?

How many people heed the warnings and take the easy, secure route? How many people allow their dreams to be dismissed because they take advice from people who are not willing to follow and live their own dreams? We've all had people tell us to lower our expectations and fall in line.

I've received the same type of messages. I've been asked countless times why I write so many blog posts and publish books since I'm (apparently) not making any money at it. I'm never asked by the play-it-safers if I'm having any success blogging and publishing books. No, possibly because they are afraid to ask – afraid to find out that following your dream can be a rewarding endeavor.

The point is that everyone has an assumption about what you should or shouldn't be doing based on *their* version of the world and how things should and shouldn't work. And since they don't believe in themselves, they also won't allow themselves to believe you can do any better. In fact, they may try to stop you. Don't let them.

"We don't see the world as it is, we see it as we are." —Anaïs Nin

However, the flipside of that is there are people who DO believe in themselves and will do everything in their power to convince you that you should believe in yourself, too.

It's no surprise why one of the above two types of people tend to become mentors and the other type of person doesn't (at least, let's hope not).

Walt Disney

Walt Disney's editor at the *Kansas City Star* newspaper fired Disney in 1919 and told him he lacked imagination and had no good ideas. What if Disney had believed him and gone on to do something more realistic and down-to-earth with his life? If so, would we have ever heard of Walt Disney?

5 Things Play-It-Safers Say to Talk You Out of Your Dreams:

1. You're not lucky enough

The reality is that you make your own luck by putting yourself in the position for opportunity to strike. Play-it-safers never get "lucky" because they never position themselves for opportunities.

If you never write and publish a book, then you never have to worry about it not selling, much less about it becoming a bestseller. However, if you do write and publish a book, you position yourself for opportunity, and to write and publish more books. Your bestseller might not be your first book. It might be your second or third.

2. You don't know the right people

The play-it-safers will never know the right people because they don't get out there to do the work and network. If you're putting yourself in the position for opportunity to strike, then you're also putting yourself in position to network with the "right" people.

3. What if it doesn't work out?

Play-it-safers will always try to make you think of the worst case scenario because that's what they focus on. The worst case scenario usually means you end up right back where you are right now.

Wow – you're going to let that stop you? I didn't think so. The worst case scenario is never as bad as someone else imagines it for you.

"I am an old man and have known a great many troubles. I have been through some terrible things in my life, some of which actually happened…" –Mark Twain

4. You will fail

The one thing you'll notice from the vast majority who try to talk you out of something is that they speak in absolutes.

You will fail. Really? How do they know that? People who never take any risks of their own cannot see the upside of trying something challenging. No one's ever accomplished something worthwhile that didn't hold the risk of "It might not work."

And so what if you do fail? Failure isn't a bad thing, especially when you learn valuable lessons you would not have learned otherwise.

5. It's hard work

Of course, following your dream is hard work, but that's not a bad thing or something to avoid. Thanks to TV and radio, we hear about overnight success stories all the time, but the truth is by the time you see someone new on TV, or hear a new artist sing on the radio, they've already been paying their dues working behind the scenes on their crafts for years.

It's always going to be hard work, and that's okay.

Remember the other type of people I mentioned who do believe in themselves and will do everything in their power to convince you that you should believe in yourself, too? Find such a person, ask him or her to coach you, to be your mentor, and get ready to roll up your sleeves. For those who follow their dreams, hard work is just another way that demonstrates it's worth it.

Don't Be a Play-It-Safer

Don't let anyone talk you out of your dream simply because they can't see or even imagine what you can see and imagine. For you the sky is not the limit, but the naysayers and play-it-safers reached their limit of mediocrity long ago.

Let the play-it-safers, play it safe. But not you!

Just About the Worst Advice You Can Give a Writer

By Bryan Hutchinson (Originally published on _Goins Writer_)

"This too shall pass." I'm sure you've heard this adage before. But what does it really mean?

Maybe you've gone through a difficult situation and someone said it to make you feel better. Or perhaps you were feeling blocked or frustrated and said it to yourself to help you persevere. Some of us even have this posted on our computer screens as a reminder of the temporary status of a situation.

This too shall pass.

I've heard it a lot lately. It's become a catchall phrase to soothe any worry or struggle a person might be experiencing. And as comforting as it seems, this is not a harmless saying. In fact, if you're a writer, it could prolong what you're going through or, heaven forbid, make it worse.

Think about it: what does "this too shall pass" mean? Waiting. And guess what? As an artist, waiting is the last thing you should do.

What are you waiting for?

Are you holding out for inspiration? Motivation? Desire? Better days to come? Maybe a deadline to pass or that last-minute surge of energy to finish a project you've been putting off?

Here's the truth: All those excuses are bogus. When you're waiting, you're not creating. You're allowing valuable time to go by, which you can never get back. It's gone… forever.

When I talk about waiting, I'm not referring to mindfulness and meditation, learning to embrace the in-between by taking a walk along the seashore on a beautiful sunshiny day. Those are helpful activities.

I'm talking about stalling.

The Doubt We All Face (and How to Overcome It)

In times of waiting, we allow our minds to wander. And too often when we do this, we begin to imagine the worst: that we aren't really artists. We're just pretending, and maybe we should give up.

After all, "this too shall pass" doesn't seem to be passing with any haste. In fact, haven't you noticed it's getting worse?

That's doubt talking.

If you wait long enough, hoping those self-defeating thoughts will evaporate, they won't. And the longer you wait, the more rooted they become. It's a trap many of us fall into.

Here's what you need to do…

Stop waiting. Because it's not helping. "This too shall pass?" Not likely. Not until you do *something*.

The good news is you can do something. You can write. It's within you to create greatness. All you have to do is start. You have the talent, the ability, and the imagination. If you start now by creating and focusing on your art, doubt will take a backseat to the power of doing something.

I've said this before and I'll say it again: You are magical.

Taking action will bring forth power within you that you didn't know was there. You can worry whether you're good enough, filling yourself with anxiety, or you can let go and start doing something that will make a difference.

You are able. You are more than good enough. You have greatness in you, wanting to come out. Doubt is loudest and at its most insidious when you do nothing. So just start moving your fingers. Doubt will retreat when you advance.

A practical plan is to start with 200 to 500 words a day. Just write what comes to mind, and when you reach your word limit and still have more to say, go ahead and keep writing.

Then do it again tomorrow, and the next day, and the next. And so on.

The Good, the Bad, and the Ugly (of Writing)

Write when it feels good and when it's hard and when the words come out all wrong. Write when you're tired and angry and unsure of your ability. As you do this, sooner or later, your message will come. What seems like gibberish today will become what you've always wanted to say but could never muster the courage to get out.

Try it. Keep writing until your message becomes clear and your voice emerges. Write your story with boldness, facing Writer's Doubt as it comes and doing it anyway. Because that's your greatness. That's your "magic," the message within you that the world needs to hear.

You're a writer, so write. That's what we do. Even when you don't know what to write about, just start. Your message will come.

Surviving Criticism without Losing Confidence in Your Writing

By Marcy McKay

When it happens, you feel like the flesh has been ripped from your body, leaving your heart exposed, helpless and raw. Shame courses through your veins. You question your talents as a writer. You wonder if you should start over, or quit altogether. The only detail you're quite sure of is how wounded you feel.

The nightmare experience I'm describing is...

Criticism

If you're going to let another living, breathing human being read your writing, then you must learn to deal with this challenge. Especially if publication is your ultimate goal.

Family, friends and complete strangers will feel they have the right to pass judgment over your work – both online and to your face.

Why Criticism Feels So Personal

Every writer knows how each word comes from deep inside you, whether it's fiction or nonfiction. You share the essence of you – your thoughts, feelings, knowledge or imagination bleeds onto the page.

You soak in praise from others, so it's hard not do the same with disapproval – to absorb the pain like a poison. If you take that negativity personally, it can destroy your self-confidence. So much so some writers never pick up a pen again. They give up on their hopes and dreams forever.

I don't want that to happen to you.

I want to help you find a better way to deal with this important part of the process because we do need feedback on our work. Both as we're still creating our art, but not ready to send it out into the world, as well as from readers after we're done. That's true whether it's just a select few you let read it, sitting on a bookshelf somewhere in a chain store, or to be downloaded online.

A Funny Thing Happened at the Conference

I've been writing for years, so I've experienced more than my fair share of jabs. In 2010, my novel, *Pennies from Burger Heaven*, won Best Mainstream Novel at the Texas Writers' League's annual manuscript contest/conference. Winning first prize meant I earned a free ten-minute meeting with the literary agent who judged my category.

I felt so proud as I stepped down from the winners' podium. The entire ballroom applauded all the winners like we were rock stars. My cell phone rang, so I stepped into the lobby to answer it. The caller was an acquaintance from my local writers' organization. Their annual conference was that same weekend, and I knew I'd won an award in their contest, but didn't know what.

She told me *Pennies* had won Best Mainstream novel.

Sweet.

She said I also won Best of Show (meaning my book won first place against all the first-prize winners).

Even better.

However, she did point out that my book did not win the Young Adult category, which she had judged, and then proceeded to tell me every detail wrong with my story.

Ouch.

The room began to spin. Her words punched my gut as if she was telling me how ugly, wretched and awful my newborn baby looked.

Fortunately, I had enough years of experience to handle the situation. Since that author does not write, read or publish YA, I just thanked her for the call and said I had to go discuss my award-winning novel with an agent, then hung up.

A Tale of Two Authors

I have two friends who are traditionally-published authors. Both women have written multiple novels and have earned six figures for their books. However, each responds to criticism quite differently.

Author #1 scours Amazon, Goodreads and anywhere else for her reviews, whether they are songs of five-star praise, or one-star haters. She laughs hysterically about the horrible remarks people make about her.

Author #2 knows her heart cannot stand to read anything less than a four-star review. It upsets her too much and affects her writing, so she limits reading about herself. (I would fall into this category, too).

Neither author is right or wrong. Each just handles the situation in her own way.

Here are three steps to help you handle criticism, while still maintaining both your dignity and your sanity.

1. Consider the Source

- Contest judges, writing instructors, professors, published authors, agents, editors, fellow writers – everyone is just expressing their opinion. Yes, pay closer attention to industry experts, those who write within your genre, or people with years of experience. They have much to teach you. However...

- There are exceptions to every rule. Even industry experts can be mistaken. I heard agents and editors once at a conference say all weekend how you should hook your readers within the first 20 pages, but then pointed out how *The Girl with the Dragon Tattoo* challenged that thinking. It was just ho-hum the first 175 pages, then exploded.

- Sadly, some people are just plain cruel. If they trash everyone, or play favorites in your writing group or class, ignore them. They have nothing helpful to offer you anyway. If possible, get as far away as possible from them.

2. Examine the Content

- Just because someone slams your writing, even in a hateful way, does not mean they are wrong, or somehow against you. This sounds like a contradiction to #1, but it's not. The problem with criticism isn't always what it said, but how it is said.

- Step back. You may need time and space for a clearer perspective from the critique. When I finally signed with a literary agent, my manuscript bled so much painful red ink, I wondered, "Does she even like my book?" No, she loved it and was trying help me make it even stronger. It took me awhile (two or three weeks of crying) to see that fact. I ended up agreeing with almost 90% of what she said and changed the parts that rang true for me.

3. Let it Go

- Easier said than done. If you cannot move on from your anger or sadness after a while (days or weeks), try writing a nasty letter to that person (which will never be sent). Tell him/her exactly how you X@#% feel! This helps release the negative energy, so you can refocus on your writing again.

- You may need to enlist assistance from those in your inner circle to help you regain perspective. They can read/listen to the comments in a calmer, more unbiased way.

Bottom Line:

Criticism can hurt and may always sting at first. Every criticism is not bad, but it may not be helpful, either. You have to measure the comments against your instincts. Only you know the true vision for your work. The secret is to not let criticism destroy your self-confidence so much that you give up on your dream altogether.

How to Give Constructive Writing Criticism (That Actually Helps)

By Marcy McKay

Since we've already discussed "Surviving Criticism without Losing Confidence in Your Writing," I thought it would be fun and helpful to also talk about the best way to give others feedback on their writing.

I recently read, *Creativity, Inc. - Overcoming the Unseen Forces that Stand in the Way of True Aspiration* by Ed Catmull, president of Pixar Animation and Disney Animation. They produced such modern-animated classics as *Toy Story, Monsters, Inc.* and *Frozen*.

I learned there are distinct differences between criticism and constructive criticism.

Catmull conveys the idea that with constructive criticism, you're constructing at the same time as you're criticizing. You're building as you're breaking down, making new pieces to work from what you just ripped apart.

It's an art form we all should learn.

Ugly Babies

Creativity, Inc. says originality is fragile. Early on, your story is far from pretty. Even if it's just page one of your someday four-hundred-page novel, your writing comes from deep inside you, and you already love it.

Catmull describes this infancy stage of your work as an "ugly baby."

How would you feel if a stranger, or worse, a friend, family member or writing mentor, saw the child snuggled in your arms and shouted, "What a Gawd-awful ugly baby! I mean, his eyes are almost crossed, and will ya look at the schnozzer on that kid? Disgusting!"

It would crush you.

Many writers feel as attached to their stories as they do to their children. Some have been so hurt by criticism that they quit the craft altogether.

It's a shame.

Be gentle when critiquing an ugly baby. Don't be responsible for ruining what could've been a beautiful story – if it had the chance to grow up.

Here are three ways to help your fellow writers without insulting them:

1. Use Candor, Not Honesty

Most everyone agrees honesty is the best policy. Nobody wants to be known as dishonest, or worse, a liar. Catmull says, "A hallmark of a healthy creative culture is that its people feel free to share ideas, opinions, and criticisms."

However, there's baggage that comes with honesty and he suggests we use candor instead. "Candor is forthrightness or frankness – not so different from honesty, really. And yet, in common usage, the word (honesty) communicates not just truth-telling, but a lack of reserve. Everyone knows that sometimes, being reserved is healthy, even necessary for survival."

Do not misunderstand me. You can argue or disagree heatedly about a story. Certainly the other person needs to know what didn't work or confused you about their writing, but you can temper your final judgment until their piece is more fully formed.

"Creativity has to start somewhere, and we (Pixar and Disney) are true believers in the power of bracing, candid feedback and the iterative process – reworking, reworking, and reworking again, until a flawed story finds its throughline or a hollow character finds its soul."

Don't insult someone's ugly baby, especially early on in the writing process. Ask questions to help authors find their story. Sometimes they're too close to their own words to achieve objectivity.

Example:

Don't say: "Nothing about this plot works. It's already been done a thousand times."

Instead, try: "I'm intrigued by this idea. At this point, what do you think the overall message is you're trying to convey? Let's brainstorm, so your story can have a really fresh twist."

The first comment is too raw and direct. The second still conveys something is off, but it isn't as disheartening.

2. Candor Isn't Cruel

If you've ever shared your writing with others, then you've probably experienced painful criticism. It hurts, doesn't it?

Catmull says when critiquing, "Your objective is not to destroy the other person. On the contrary, successful feedback is built on empathy...we understand your pain because we've experienced it before."

Yes, it's important to be candid about where someone's writing needs improvement, but it's not just what you say, it's how you say it.

Example:

Don't say: "The dialogue in this scene isn't realistic. Nobody talks boring like that."

Instead, try: "I like you're characters, but I know you want people quoting your novel long after they've read it. Let's brainstorm ways to bring your dialogue alive."

The first comment falls flat and doesn't help. The second still says something is wrong, but is much more open and encouraging.

3. Start with the Positive

This last suggestion is mine, not Catmull's. Whenever I hear someone slam my work, it's hard for me to not shut down. Sometimes, I don't hear another word after that initial cruel punch.

When offering feedback to others, I try to find at least one aspect I like about the writing and start there. Yes, it was a challenge, but it was always early on in the author's story when he/she was still finding their way.

Try to treat others writers the way you want to be treated (The Golden Rule, baby).

Example:

Don't say: "Your main character is static. As a reader, I don't care what happens to her."

Instead, try: "I'm intrigued by your character. Keep working on her (her goals, motivation and conflict), so that she comes across as more three-dimensional and real."

Recap - Constructive Criticism

1. Yes, writers need to hear what's wrong with their work in order to improve it, but there's a positive way and a negative way to convey that message.

2. It's not just what you say, it's how you say it.

3. Constructive criticism, done right, leaves the receiver excited to make revisions to their story, rather than feeling shattered.

Why You Need to Shut Up and Write!

By Bryan Hutchinson

I've been stuck lately. Way stuck. Lost-in-the-Amazon jungle, stuck. And that's stuck, my friends. If you need to use the word stuck five or six times within your first few sentences, then that's, well, pretty stuck. Yup. I hate to admit it, but I've been without a fresh idea to write about for months. But that's all changed because I've rediscovered a well-kept secret.

The problem started with the completion of my latest book. The book had been in the works for the last few years and had kept me so busy writing that I didn't need to force myself to think up any fresh ideas because they were pouring out of me onto the page already. (Don't you love when that happens?)

When the project was finally completed it was a time for celebration and I felt a wonderful sense of release and accomplishment, but it also brought with it the dreaded void. I became lost as to what to write about next.

Perhaps you've experienced the "Idea Void" phenomenon after completing a major writing project, too?

I always need to be doing something. I need to have my fingers moving, typing – clickety-clack. I need to be exploiting an idea. So I started to:

- Brainstorm.
- Ask everyone I knew for ideas and suggestions.

- Read more blog posts and magazine articles, and listened to more audio books.
- Still nothing... until I...

Shut Up!

My thoughts were alphabet soup in my head, swirling around like a tornado. That's what happens when you panic and get desperate for ideas. You don't have an idea, but you're a writer, and you need to write about something, so when you draw a blank you start to freak out. You know better, but you do it anyway. (Go ahead, admit it. It's ok.)

Stop. Quiet your mind. The answer isn't in forcing yourself into thinking up new ideas or putting any kind of additional pressure on yourself because that will just have the opposite affect and cause you to get brainlocked.

Brainlock is an internal message that you need to take a break and regroup, so your mind shuts down in order to force your hand.

Here are a few steps to help you get back to writing sooner, rather than later:

Step 1: After finishing a major project, congratulate yourself for a job well done!

Step 2: Go celebrate! Perhaps take a trip, or eat ice cream (I prefer chocolate), or have a party. Basically, do something that's very special to you.

Step 3: Instead of forcing yourself to think of something new, relax. The ideas will come, so there's no need to force them. The more you panic and force yourself to come up with ideas the longer it will be before you start writing again.

Step 4: Change up your routine, which leads me to...

Silence

For the last few years while working on *Writer's Doubt*, it was there every morning waiting for me. I'd wake up, go make some coffee, and head to my desk knowing what I would write about that day.

Knowing what you're going to write about is half the battle.

Not having a project waiting for me each morning left me more than a little bewildered. Until I remembered the secret of... *silence*.

Silence is from where the greatest ideas, innovations and inventions, and especially, the greatest writings, first come into being.

You know how it is. You're not thinking of anything of relevance and suddenly a great idea pops into your head and you have no idea where it came from. It's when we calm down and STOP forcing ourselves to think that our minds are truly free to process our thoughts and deliver to us that which we seek.

"Never miss a good chance to shut up." —Will Rogers

New Routine

Now I have a modified routine every morning and I follow it even when I already have a clear idea of what I want to write about for the day.

I wake up, make the coffee, and then sit at my writing desk and stop all thinking for the next 5 minutes. 5 minutes of silence is all I need to rejuvenate my spirit for writing. Silence truly is golden. When we are silent we are able to tap into our subconscious, and at the same time, release anxiety and stress, and just be.

It's in moments of silence that the best ideas surface and make themselves known to us, which will lead us into our natural creative flow. If you haven't tried it yet, give it a chance. Don't worry about completely shutting off your thoughts — that's not possible — but it is possible to ignore them and focus on the quietness within.

5 quick tips on using silence to generate ideas:

1. Pick a time and place where you won't be interrupted.

2. Sit down and make sure you're comfortable.

3. Close your eyes and with your mind's eye visualize something to anchor your focus. For example, I like to focus on the calm surface of a lake.

4. As thoughts try to interrupt you, simply acknowledge them, but don't engage with them. Let them go.

5. When you're finished, immediately write down any ideas that come to you over the next few minutes and if one appeals to you more than the others, consider writing more details about it.

5 Minutes

Take 5 minutes of your time today and simply sit in silence. Who knows, you may come up with your next blog post, an essay idea for your contest entry, or maybe even an idea for your next book.

Let's procrastinate…

8 Reasons Why Procrastinating Is Better than Working

By Bryan Hutchinson

Don't you hate wasting time? You need to get to it and do the work. But what if forcing yourself to do the work isn't always the best answer? What if doing so will result in long-lasting creative blocks? On the other hand, procrastination could hold unlimited potential for your sanity, overall well-being, and productivity.

I've become prolific because I learned the value of procrastination. I stopped fighting it and gave into it wholeheartedly. Procrastination could be the key to unlocking your creative flow, too.

I love creating stuff that matters, and I like to think I've been rather successful, but there are times when I just I don't feel like it. I'd rather be doing something else, even if it's just daydreaming, or, as too many others see it, procrastinating.

I'm cool with that. And yet I'm one of the most productive people I know. Seems kind of odd doesn't it?

Maybe not.

I've talked with others I know who are extremely productive, more so than I am, and all have admitted they don't buy into the "work your butt off" mentality. It's liberating and allows one the freedom to remove unnecessary pressure that otherwise would inhibit one's creative flow.

I've spent the last two weeks not writing and I don't feel the least bit guilty about it, and I don't feel guilty for not feeling guilty about it. Here's the thing: when I force myself to write, I end up with work I don't appreciate or I spend hours staring at a screen until my eyes are about to pop out.

That's wasting time! And it is stressful. Procrastinating is better than spending time stressing myself out.

Creative types, especially writers, are famous for giving the advice to sit down and do the work even if you don't feel like it. I'm guilty of it, too. However, the mind needs down time, it needs time to ponder, and even time to recover. If we are always going, going, going, forcing ourselves when our mind and body are telling us to rest, then we'll just end up getting nowhere faster and probably crash somewhere along the way.

If we are creating just anything for the sake of staying busy, we are more likely to be unhappy, miserable, and dissatisfied with the results. So why do we force ourselves anyway? Let's put a stop to the madness.

I discovered that the more time I put off writing and procrastinate, the more time I spend creating. It goes against everything I've ever been taught, but it works.

How's that possible?

The short answer is: remember The Tortoise and the Hare? You can still win by taking your time.

The long answer is:

1. You'll create work that matters to you

Today we are all about working to meet deadlines, to get things done and then do more and more. It's excess. And what we ultimately end up doing is burning out early and often. Downtime allows you to recharge your mind, body, and soul. Recharged we create work that matters, that feels satisfying and worthwhile.

If you don't feel like creating right now, that's okay. Go for a walk, go to a movie, or take a nap. When you're ready to create, you'll know it, and you'll do a better job that you will appreciate.

2. You'll be less stressed

Procrastination helps release stress. Stress is not only counter-creative, it is destructive. 77% of people regularly experience physical symptoms caused by stress. To be at your most creative you need to be relaxed, stress free, and ready and willing to enjoy the creative process.

3. You'll produce more

Procrastination enables you to produce more by giving your brain time to take in and organize your thoughts, all that you have learned and researched. If the brain is always going from one task to another, it doesn't have time to refresh and allow thoughts to settle for further reflection.

4. You'll be happier

By taking time off from the creative process, you'll find there are other things to enjoy than just your butt aching in a chair and your eyes getting sore from staring at the blank page on a computer screen. The world is full of wonder and awe. Go explore it and come back and write about it, paint what you saw, or sculpt something that caught your eye and inspired you.

5. You'll have more quality time for your loved ones

My wife loves going to the zoo and visiting historical places, and so do I. But all too often, I put off a day trip to stay home and write (to "do the work" as it were). I've wasted too many days forcing myself to write when I didn't feel like it, and I ended up producing stuff I wasn't happy with.

I don't do that anymore. Instead, I get up, turn the PC off, and take my wife somewhere wonderful. Watching her smile ignites my creative passion anew, and when we get home I'm usually ready and willing to write stuff that matters to me (and hopefully my readers!).

6. It's easier

We've come to a point in history when we believe everything must be ever more challenging in order to create wonderful work.

Procrastination is easy to do. The mind needs to know that "easy" is okay and not everything has to be a challenge to be worthwhile.

7. Your natural creativity will flow

Whenever you force yourself to create you're not allowing your natural creativity to flow. You're taking a "short cut" up the steep side of the mountain and it'll take you ten times as long to get to the top than taking the winding path that leads leisurely to the top. Worse, you might give up because the path is too treacherous and exhausting.

It doesn't have to be that way.

There's nothing wrong with a good challenge and putting in some hard work, but the point is that we can only go, go, go so long before we reach the point of diminishing returns.

8. You'll have time to eat healthier

When you're constantly busy there's little time to eat properly. When I pushed myself to create, I constantly munched on gummy bears, popcorn and pop tarts, and drank plenty of coffee to wash them down. By taking the time I deserve to relax and restore myself, I eat healthier food and more slowly. I actually enjoy my meals now. Overall I feel much better and when I sit down to create, I'm ready, willing and able, with energy to spare.

I've chosen to make procrastination something that works for me, not against me.

The problem is that too often when we take a break and are not doing some kind of work we call it procrastination. It's always been a dreadful word none of us want to be accused of. We'll overwork ourselves to the point of burning out before we allow ourselves to be seen as procrastinating.

Let's be honest. Forcing ourselves to stay busy doesn't mean we'll produce more or that what we produce will be quality work. No. More likely we'll be silently resentful of all the time we spent staying busy and missing out on life. Maybe not today, maybe not tomorrow, but the day will come.

I say embrace procrastination and you'll waste less time, and you'll be energized when you do feel like creating. And you'll still get your 200 or 500 words a day, probably more.

Procrastination is a word. Powerful, maybe, but it only has the meaning and power you give it.

As humans, we are meant to relax and do things to free ourselves from the daily grind so we can regenerate. Sleep, relaxation, and play are built into our DNA! The fact is we can be way too hard on ourselves and force ourselves into creative blocks if we don't listen to our mind and body. If you've been feeling blocked for days on end, it might be that your mind is overworked, your body is exhausted, and they are telling you something.

Listen to them.

Sounds like it's time for some quality procrastination.

The Bulletproof Guide to Free Writing

By Bryan Collins of *Become a Writer Today*

I'm stuck. This isn't any good. I can't think of an idea.

Almost every practicing writer faces these negative thoughts at one stage or another. If you're struggling with writer's block, if your internal editor is holding you back, or if your current writing project is troublesome, there is a solution.

It's called free writing.

It's a writing technique during which writers express their ideas without caring if they make sense, how they are spelt, or even if they are usable. Free writing can help you overcome problems like writer's block and self-criticism. It's also a type of writing practice that any writer can benefit from, no matter their experience.

If you'd like to free write, these ten tips will help you get started:

1. Write without editing yourself

Free writing only works if you don't question or criticize every sentence, idea and story that you put down on the blank page. Instead, let the words flow freely from your fingers onto the page without pausing or questioning what you are saying.

Then, when you've finished your free writing for the day, spend time polishing, buffing and making your prose shine.

2. Time your free writing sessions

To get the most from free writing, apply this technique during concentrated, sustained and timed bursts of creativity.

Get a clock (or the timer on your computer), set it for twenty-five minutes and write. Then, when the buzzer sounds, take a short break and repeat. Do this two to four times before taking a longer break.

3. Write whatever comes to mind

Free writing enables you to follow a train of thought in new and exciting directions. Some of these directions may be dead-ends, but they're still worth exploring.

When you're free writing, record what you're thinking or if you feel distracted – it doesn't matter if it's unrelated to the topic you're writing about. This could mean recording the sound of a dog on the street, the color of a plant on your desk, or even a swear word.

Don't hold back.

4. Free write for an hour or longer

This is a tough tip for writers to implement. If you're struggling to make a breakthrough, free write for an extended period without taking a break. Your job is to keep going until you make a break-through.

Yes, this is mentally and physically demanding but you don't have to do it very often, and it will help you break through those difficult barriers every writer faces at some point.

5. Keep your hand moving

This is straight from the pages of Natalie Goldberg's excellent book *Writing Down the Bones: Freeing the Writer Within*. An advocate of free writing, or writing practice as she calls it, she recommends "keeping your hand moving."

If you're a typist, don't take your fingers from the keys until you're finished writing. If you prefer a pen, this means keeping the pen pressed between your fingers. And if you like to dictate your writing, keep the Dictaphone recording until you're done.

6. Keep a list of topics to free write about

I use Evernote to organize my writing. Inside Evernote, I keep a notebook full of topics that I want to free write about. Examples include ideas for short stories, sentence fragments, blog posts and ideas that I want to expand on.

Then when I want to free write, I pick one item from my notebook and go with it. Keeping these types of lists means I spend less time looking for a topic and more time free writing.

7. Combine free writing with other types of writing

Free writing is just one writing technique you can employ to advance your work.

There are times when it makes more sense to plan your writing in advance or aim towards a target word count. Combining free writing with other types of writing sessions will help you mix things up during the week, test your boundaries, and avoid becoming bored with the process.

8. Keep your cast-offs

Free writing also produces a lot of leftover ideas and copy that doesn't immediately belong anywhere. Whatever you do, don't throw this writing in the bin or delete it. Instead, keep your cast-offs in your journal or a file on your computer.

There will come a time when it makes sense to return to these leftovers and extract something useful from them. And even if this time never comes, they serve as markers for your progress as a writer over time.

9. Read a book in your niche, take an idea from it and expand

I read a lot of non-fiction books. This means I regularly come across ideas that surprise me, inspire me or confound me. Sometimes, I take these ideas and expand on them during free writing sessions. Free writing about ideas helps me internalize them and figure out how I can apply them to my creative life.

If you want to do the same, underline key passages in the books you are reading, write notes in the margins, and review these notes when you're finished with the book. Then, pick one or two ideas and use these for your next free writing sessions.

10. Free write a problem upside down

Are you having trouble with a particularly writing project? Perhaps the feedback from a client isn't helpful. Or maybe you can't figure out the right arc for a short story. Write down this problem at the top of your page. Now free write everything about the problem that's bothering you and even what you're afraid of. Then, free write all the solutions you can think of. It doesn't matter how preposterous, outlandish or impractical they sound. If you get lucky, you'll make a breakthrough and even if you don't, you are still venting your frustrations and practice writing at the same time.

Why You Should Free Write For Kicks

As a writer, there are times when you need to reach your goals, hit a word count and press publish. There are other times when writing is supposed to be fun, when you need to try something different or when you must go in a new direction.

For these other times, free writing is the perfect writing technique. This week, allocate 30 minutes of time you usually spend writing, and use it to free write about whatever you want. If it helps, think of free writing as a guilty pleasure. Who knows where you'll end up.

How to Silence Negative Voices and Write

By Josh Irby of *JoshIrby.com*

My children are inquisitive. When I am driving they ask at least one question per minute. Sometimes, their questions come so quickly and loudly I cannot hear my own thoughts. I feel like my brain is being hijacked.

Often, when I sit down to write, I feel the same way. I try to engage my mind with the world of words but my mind is under new management. I am no longer in control.

In this case, however, the voices are not those of my children. They are voices from within. Silencing those voices is my secret to finding my creative flow. Internal negative voices come in many forms.

- There is the Critic—"That's not good enough."
- There is the Cynic—"No one is going to read it."
- There is the Doubter—"Perhaps writing is not for you."
  And, of course, all of their friends.

These voices take up residence in our minds and prevent us from creating. If we want to release our writing voice we must silence these squatters. Here is how I silence the voices in my head:

Recognize the Voice

At first, all my internal voices sound like my own. They sound like my thoughts. However, when I listen closely, I discover something different. Most of these voices actually come from people around me—

friends, family, teachers, leaders. One voice I regularly hear as I sit down to write says, "You're not a writer. You are just faking it. Shouldn't you be using your time for something more productive?"

It is really hard to create something compelling with this message echoing in my brain. But, as I have given attention to the voice, I recognized it. It sounds familiar.

When I was in high school I met with my guidance counselor to talk about college options. She asked me what subjects I enjoyed. I told her I liked Biology and Math. She swiveled in her chair and looked in her big book of careers. Rotating back towards me she said, "You should be a Biomedical Engineer."

And so I went to engineering school.

Today, 20 years later, when I sit down to write, my old guidance counselor swivels around in my mind, looks in her book, and asks, "Writing? That's not what it says in my book." I have allowed her to take residence in my mind. She drones on and on, "You are not a writer, you're an engineer." And because of her voice, I struggle to call myself a writer. But now that I recognize her voice, I am on the way to evicting her completely.

There is power in calling something by its real name.

Reject the Voice

Once I recognize the voice, I speak back.

Here is where we get a little psychoanalytical. As long as that person has power over me, that voice will have power over me. I need to let them know that they don't own me and can't tell me what to do.

What relevance does my high school guidance counselor have on my life today? Only the relevance I allow her to have.

What power does a voice have in your life? Only the power you allow it to have.

- Don't allow a bully from middle school to still determine how you view yourself.
- Don't allow a side comment from a parent to overshadow the truth.
- Don't allow a past failure to lead you into failure today.
- Don't allow one discouraging person to prevent you from getting your work out to the thousands who will be encouraged by it.

Reject the voice.

Note: This might require hard conversations with real people. This might require a little confrontation. This might require discomfort. But how much is your freedom worth? It's sure hard to create with unwanted guests living in your mind.

Replace the Voice with the Truth

Just because I remove a voice one day does not mean it will not come back the next. To rid myself of negative inner voices I must replace them with the truth.

The truth:

- My guidance counselor did not create me.
- She did not determine my gifts and talents.
- She is not God's representative to dictate my life's direction.
- If God gave me the desire and skill to write, then I should write.

That's the truth. And, the truth, when spelled out, is powerful.

Now, I am not talking about made up, wishful mantras. Just saying "I'm the best writer ever!" does not make it true. The truth is, you're probably not. Neither am I. There are many who write better than you and I. When we use this wishful thinking, we only replace a lie with a lie.

It's like drinking a Coke. Sure, you will get a burst of energy, but it can't sustain you. But there is truth that sustains:

- You are a unique creation.
- No one writes exactly like you.
- If you don't write, you cheat the world of your voice.
- There are readers waiting for your writing. You just have to write and find them.

That's the truth.

When you recognize, reject, and replace the negative voices in your head, you will discover the beauty of a quiet mind. And your unique voice will flow out onto the page.

6 Weird but Awesome Hacks for a Happy Writing Life

By Shanan Haislip

Whether you're a full-time writer, a hobby writer, or a writer with another full-time job, you have to admit that being a writer is a pretty good life. On the whole, we're pretty lucky to do what we love. But...

But like any lifestyle, it's got some rough spots, some things that need to be smoothed out. Such as:

6. Get your writing juices flowing early with writing podcasts

Writing podcasts are a way to instantly connect with your writing self, whether it's 6:30am or 9:30pm. As a writer with another full-time job, I write early in the morning, late at night, and on weekends, but I still have trouble just jumping right into the writing mindset when I've just rolled out of bed, or when I'm tired.

But when I turn on the Writing University podcast, hosted at the University of Iowa, I can always find a topic that gets me excited for words, even before my first cup of coffee.

5. Mechanical pencils are where it's at

If you like to write in long-hand, you know that every writing implement has its issues. Gel pens get clogged, ballpoint pens get stuck and pencils make your hands smell like graphite and kindergarten.

But consider the mechanical pencil for a moment. Unless you pump out the graphite point too far (user error), mechanical pencils will never fail you. They're smooth like a ballpoint pen, easy to see like a gel pen and best of all, they're erasable.

I know we all like the cachet of writing with pens, but for absolutely hassle-free writing, consider the humble mechanical pencil. It's pretty awesome.

4. Writing in a coffeeshop? Bring cash.

Unfortunately, I learned this one from experience, and I'm a slow learner. Mostly, I write at the coffee table in my downstairs family room, but I love to write at the local Starbucks when I get the chance. (No indie coffeeshops in my fair rural town.)

However, developing coffeeshop-dwelling habits can get pretty expensive unless you plan ahead. Leave your debit card at home, and bring only exactly the amount of cash you plan to spend while you're at the coffee shop, and no more.

3. Keep your preferred hot beverage hot without leaving your writing spot

Mr. Coffee makes a USB coffee mug warmer. Use it for coffee, use it for tea, use it to keep yourself in your writing chair and not walking back and forth to the microwave to warm up your java when it gets cold. Just use it. It's convenient and ensures that a cold cup will never again break your concentration.

2. Put distance between yourself and the Internet

If you're the kind of writer who can't get through a paragraph without compulsively opening a browser window (hi! I'm one of you), this tip is for you. Freedom is a software program (it costs $10 - no affiliation) that will not allow you to access the Internet for a set period of time while you're writing.

For more low-tech solutions to this problem, unplug your Wi-Fi. I know this seems harsh, but sometimes unplugging it is the best way to break yourself of the browser-opening habit. Eventually, you'll be able to leave the browser window alone when writing. It's just going to sting a little bit.

1. Schedule breaks slightly more often than you need them

My ambition works against me when I'm trying to hit a writing goal. If I say to myself, "I'm going to sit in this chair and not get up for two hours," I know I'm setting myself up for failure.

I need breaks about every 30 minutes or I'll run out of writing steam, so I set a timer for 20 minutes, and take the break while I'm still excited about what I'm writing. This is a variation of Ernest Hemingway's famous advice to stop your writing midsentence, while you still know exactly what's going to happen next, so that the next time you sit down to write, you can pick up your momentum where you left off. Same idea.

How to Inspire Your Writing… Now!

By Bryan Hutchinson (Originally published on *The Writer Practice*)

There have been too many days when I didn't know what to write about. I sat here waiting… waiting… waiting, but nothing came to me. I used to think that some mornings I just wasn't meant to write anything. Inspiration did not visit me, and instead, I spent hours drinking cold coffee while staring blankly at my computer screen.

Well, frankly, that sucked. So I started something new. Now when I am totally stuck, instead of waiting for inspiration to strike (and when I'm not purposely procrastinating), I pick a random quote and start writing about it. I love quotes. Who doesn't?

Here's the quote for this post:

"Argue for your limitations and sure enough, they're yours." – Richard Bach

You're better than you think you are. It doesn't matter where you are in your life right now. You were meant for more!

You are more.

The human spirit within you urges you every morning to get up and create something, anything, and you want to. You need to. The problem comes when you don't think you have anything to write, paint or design that matters. That whatever you create won't be good enough to be accepted and appreciated.

When those thoughts start to take root and turn into beliefs, nothing anyone says will change your mind. You start feeling lesser than others, incapable of being more, and you start to believe that you will never achieve greatness.

The fact is: that's not true. But I am not here to convince you. I am here to help you realize:

Whatever you argue for will be (and is) true for you.

If you think you're not good enough, if you think you can't create something that matters, and if you believe in your heart of hearts no one will appreciate your work, well, then, that's your reality.

So consider this:

If you think you are good enough, that you can create something that matters, and you believe in your heart of hearts that people will appreciate your work, well, then that's your reality.

You choose.

10 Ways to Leave Your Comfort Zone and Write

By Nicole Gulotta of *Eat This Poem*

When you feel like you can't write another word, or the words you are writing don't feel fresh and inspiring, it's time to leave your comfort zone.

Creative ruts happen to us all, from writers with several books under their belts, to first-time bloggers. Because we can't expect to live in a constant stream of creative energy, ruts are merely a byproduct of the writing life, and they're unavoidable. The key is knowing how to crawl out of one and come out the other side feeling refreshed and inspired to tackle your next project, or follow-through on your current project. They're not caused by anything we do or don't do, just a byproduct of the life of a writer.

Since a new year just began, there's no better time to try something new and see where it leads you. If you're feeling stalled, here are some tips:

1. Read a book from another genre

If you're a playwright, read a novel. If you're in the middle of writing a memoir, read a book of poetry. The new perspective and fresh language might inspire you. If you're up for an exercise, borrow the first line of a novel chapter or poem and just start writing to see where you end up.

2. Read a book from another discipline

Instead of reading how-to books for writers, peruse a book about painting, history, or how to be a better photographer. Sometimes being exposed to other disciplines can rejuvenate your own.

3. Try a new cuisine

Writers need to eat. If you're always frequenting Italian restaurants, make a reservation for Cuban or Indian next time. Let the experience be sensory. What do you smell and taste? If you arrive for dinner with an open mind, you might leave with a new idea for a short story, or insights to a potential new character.

4. Explore your town

Think you've experienced everything your town has to offer? There's probably a new neighborhood, coffee shop, or attraction you haven't visited yet. Spend a weekend afternoon playing tourist in your backyard.

5. Escape

If you can manage a weekend getaway, the thrill of exploring a new city for the first time is sure to inspire. You don't have to fly across country or to an exotic destination, either. See what cities are within a 2 hour drive and start planning.

6. Visit a museum

Museums are full of potential when it comes to expanding your creativity, especially when new shows are always coming to town. Bring a notebook, sit in front of something that moves you, and listen.

7. Exercise differently

If you always attend a spin class on Monday and Wednesday nights, try Zumba or yoga instead. Logging miles on the pavement? Pack a

The Audacity to be a Writer | www.PositiveWriter.com

picnic and go for a hike. Especially when you get outdoors, the views alone can breathe new life into your projects and help you find clarity on something as small as a word or sentence that wasn't sitting well with you.

8. Buy a new notebook

This one works every time. There's something invigorating about brainstorming on a blank page where anything is possible.

9. Network

If you're the kind of writer who prefers to go through the day without so much as a single interaction with another person, you're missing out on new opportunities and relationships. Reach out to someone you recently met and would like to know better. This can be a colleague you met at a conference, fellow blogger, or friend of a friend. They don't have to be writers, just someone who you're inspired by in some way. The more you talk to other creative people, the more your ideas will take shape, not to mention that it's invigorating to be around other people who are passionate about their work.

10. Read and/or listen to author interviews

Bryan Hutchinson conducted some great interviews for you to read on Positive Writer with: Jeff Goins, Seth Godin, Joe Bunting and Guy Kawasaki.

This is the kind of list that doesn't need to be fulfilled all at once. Pick your favorite suggestion and give it a try. Also, try to go easy on yourself! The words will come again, they always do.

9 Tips on How to Totally Crush the Block

By Bryan Hutchinson

I've read far too many times that Writer's Block doesn't exist. And I've even read that because there wasn't a word for it before the 1900's, it can't exist. You know, I'm sure there was a time when there wasn't a word for "fire," but that didn't stop it from burning down forests.

Writer's Block exists. Let's get that out in the open before we delve into how to totally crush it.

Writer's Block History and Origin:

Although there hasn't always been a specific catch phrase for what we now call "Writer's Block," it is a well-documented phenomenon throughout the history of writing. In fact, the poem, "The Bells" by Edgar Allan Poe, written in 1846, originated because Poe was suffering from an inability to write at the time. Poe complained the bells ringing in the street outside were bothering him, so it was suggested that he write a poem about the bells and he did just that. (Credit: *Edgar Allan Poe: A Biography* by Milton Meltzer.)

"Biting my truant pen, beating myself for spite: "Fool!" said my muse to me, "look in thy heart, and write." By Philip Sidney, describing writer's block in *Astrophel and Stella,* composed sometime in the 1580's.

Although many websites list origin dates for the term, ranging from the 1930's to the 1950's, none of the dates I found on those sites were accurate. However, a book finally solved the date-of-origin mystery, "Writer's Block" the actual phrase was coined by psychoanalyst Edmund

Bergler in 1947. (Credit: *Comprehensive Dictionary of Psychoanalysis* By Salman Akhtar.)

"Every writer I know has trouble writing." – Joseph Heller

Writer's Block or Something Else?

To all the writers in the world who have been so fortunate to evade writer's block, good for you. Congratulations! But let me say this: Just because you might not need glasses to read doesn't mean I can take mine off and never use them again. Besides, I find the claim quite peculiar, because I've never met a human being so perfect that she's never gotten stuck, ever. Maybe you don't call it Writer's Block. That's okay. And for the rest of us that do call it Writer's Block, well, you know what? That's okay, too.

Sometimes you simply get stuck and stop writing for seemingly no reason at all. Sometimes the words don't come as easy as they did before. There's nothing wrong with that and if it happens to you, there's nothing wrong with you. Getting stuck is a natural and absolutely normal part of being human. You're not weird because you've gotten stuck, and admitting it doesn't make you a freak or any lesser of a writer.

If you've suffered from Writer's Block, that's because...

You ARE a writer!

Writer's Block is an affirmation that you are a writer. Maybe it's not an affirmation you want to repeat every day, but it's an affirmation none the less.

Only non-writers can avoid the dreaded block.

I used to get Writer's Block a lot and there were times when it lasted for years. Once, it lasted an entire decade! (True story. I share the story about how and why that happened in *Writer's Doubt*.)

I still get writer's block, but not nearly as often. Thankfully, I've learned how to overcome it. In this post, I will share 9 actionable strategies you can start using now.

Writer's Block certainly exists; in fact, there are many types:

- You've run out of ideas. You're drawing a blank because you need to do research, brainstorm or ask for help.
- You simply need a break. You've been writing nonstop for days, weeks or months (or mere minutes) and you really need down time, but you refuse to admit it so your brain shuts down on its own and won't restart until it's ready. Try to jump start it all you want, but you'll just get gibberish.
- Burn out. You don't just need a break – you need a vacation to Tahiti!
- It's not fun anymore. Sometimes we take the fun out of writing because we're too hard on ourselves, or we become overly serious and stop writing altogether because our writing gets stale and feels too much like a hopeless chore to continue. If this sounds familiar, reflect on why you started writing and recapture your true, raw passion for writing.

There are many others. The one I want to talk about today is the worst block of all, because it's the one that has proven to be my most formidable nemesis:

D O U B T

Writer's Doubt, that is!

I call it Writer's Doubt because as writers we have the unique ability to see our worst fears and most degrading thoughts come alive in our writing. If they don't present themselves in our writing, they block us from writing by constantly interrupting us as we are typing, saying things like:

"You know that isn't any good. It sucks. Admit it."

"Do you think you're an expert or something? Who are you trying to fool? Yourself? It's working."

"Your readers are going to see straight through you – oh, wait, what readers? Ha! As if! Get a life."

9 Tips on How to CRUSH Writer's Block

1. Admit you get stuck from time to time

If you're one of those who does not believe Writer's Block exists, or you have another name for it, that's fine, but I am sure you're reading this for a reason. The first step to overcoming anything is admitting that it's an issue. Some might believe denial is the best course of action; however, in reality this only prolongs the time in which you're stuck.

You're a writer and writers get stuck. So does everyone else in just about any endeavor. It's normal, so lighten up and...

2. Admit that it's okay to get stuck

Really, it is. You're human and not a machine. Most people would tell you to start writing gibberish and that will kick start your writing, and maybe that's true, sometimes. But when it doesn't work, we just tend to get more frustrated and we sink deeper into the quicksand that is doubt.

It's okay to get stuck and it's probably just an indication you need to...

3. Take a break

In a day job, breaks and lunches are mandatory for a reason. We all need to take breaks. Again, we are not machines, and yet, for some reason, we writers tend to remain sitting in front of our computers without so much as a potty break for as long as we can hold it (okay, maybe that's just me), even if we are doing no more than staring at a blank page.

Staring at the blank page or flipping through web pages, isn't usually going to inspire you to write any sooner. A break, on the other hand, might be what you need. I believe in many cases, Writer's Block is a form of mental exhaustion, so go find something to do that doesn't require serious thinking.

4. Don't self-deprecate!

In your frustration, do not start cursing yourself for not writing. You know what I am talking about. Putting extra pressure on ourselves in the form of self-deprecation won't help. The best writers are usually confident writers, so putting yourself down for being stuck won't help the way you hope it will. Oh, it might help once or twice, but that's a trick doubt plays on us.

By believing deprecation works, we'll find ourselves doing it again and again, and eventually we'll start to believe what we are saying and that's when you really get stuck. I'm talking 20-feet-in-quicksand stuck.

5. Know that you're better than you think you are

Being stuck in writer's block doesn't take anything away from your ability to write work that matters. So reinforce your confidence with truth, and affirm that you are a writer and your words make a difference. (They really do and that's why we need them.)

6. Don't describe yourself as a suffering artist

Don't ever call yourself such a thing. When you write you are creating, and that's M A G I C A L. If you want to crush Writer's Block, take control of your internal turmoil and get a firm grip on your fears and doubts. The only way to do that is to stop giving your fears and doubts control by becoming confident and self-assured.

Think about it. The role fear and doubt play in our lives is that of stealing our confidence, so don't let them. Don't fall for the belief that you need to drink alcohol, overeat, or think less of yourself so that you can write. You don't need to do any of those things to create work that matters, but fear and doubt can make you believe otherwise.

7. Be audacious

Whatever you're afraid of writing, write it. In my experience, when I hold back, I get stuck. Don't hold back. You can't make a difference or create work that matters if you're not willing to say what you want to say. Say it. Say it with confidence. If you're trying to tip toe around the truth then you're not really saying what matters to you. Keep in mind it is not always necessary to share all of your work, but at least write it out for yourself if for no one else.

8. Accept discouragement as part of the writer's life, but do not give in to despair

All of us get discouraged. ALL OF US. It's a natural and normal part of life and it will pass.

However, for writers it is too easy for discouragement to turn into despair. One of the reasons for this is that we sit for long periods of time alone with our thoughts. Alone with our thoughts anything can happen, especially when we are stuck and do not realize our negative thoughts are running amok.

The best way to crush Writer's Block is to never give in to despair and never give up on writing.

If you realize you are starting to feel overly discouraged consider talking about it with someone who understands what you are going through, such as with a trusted friend, coach, or mentor. Also consider writing in a personal journal about how you feel. This might seem like odd advice, but you may find that you can write in a personal journal even while in the midst of writer's block. Writing in a journal for one's self can be cathartic, revealing, and liberating.

9. Accept yourself (and your writing) as you are right now

There's plenty of room for all of us to improve and become better writers, but the problem comes when we get caught up in the never-ending cycle of self-improvement, and we hold back our best work. Some of us believe our work is not good enough until we reach a certain milestone, but more often than not, we don't have a clue what that milestone is.

All of us should strive to become better writers, but if you're using that as an excuse not to ship your best work now, you might never ship. Whatever your best work is right now, there will come a time when you will look back on it and realize you could have done better, and you might tell yourself you should have waited. Don't fall into that trap.

All (wise) authors know they could have done better. That's part of writing and constantly moving forward. It takes great emotional effort to publish our best work now.

The Secret

"When words don't come easy, I make do with silence and find something in nothing." –Strider Marcus Jones

We all need time to pause, to reflect, to take action, and to be audacious. The secret is not giving in to frustration and admitting to yourself what it is you really need when you're stuck. Simply ask yourself what you need, and if you're calm and quiet for a moment or two, I'm sure you'll come up with the answer.

I've heard many writers state that after they've suffered from Writer's Block and begun to write again, they found that they had somehow made a quantum leap forward with their writing! I've experienced this, too.

Writer's Block can be a positive indication you're about to have a massive breakthrough.

Why So Many Blogs and Books Utterly and Completely Fail!

By Bryan Hutchinson

Yesterday I watched one of the weirdest, most unprofessional, and perhaps the dumbest YouTube videos ever. Then I looked at the number of views, and it has to date over 28 million views. Okay, I've changed my mind; it's brilliant.

Most of the highest grossing movies of the year will be panned by critics, much less considered for an award by the Academy of Motion Picture Arts and Sciences, and yet they will earn more money than you and I could earn in ten lifetimes. And they'll likely earn far more than the actual winners of academy awards.

Who is fooling who? It's a travesty! Isn't it? Maybe not.

There's a blog I love. It is one of the most read on the net about positive thinking, and yet it's riddled with grammar and spelling mistakes. Although the author writes in English, it's clearly her second language. But you know what? It doesn't matter, not to me and certainly not to her 60,000 readers. (I should link to her blog, but she might take it the wrong way, so I'll keep it anonymous for this post.)

The reason many blogs and books utterly fail is that while the authors are trying their best to write as "perfectly" as possible, they overlook the reality that most readers don't care as much about literary perfection as some in the industry would have them believe.

It's not perfection they should be striving for. By focusing on being perfect (and approved of), they fail where it matters most, and that's in creating a connection with their readers.

Hunger Games and *Twilight*

I read about highbrow critics and literary purists tearing down books like *Hunger Games* and *Twilight* because they say those books are not "well written."

Reality check: Their audience doesn't care. And no matter how many times certain people stamp their feet and scream in outrage, that isn't going to change. So does this mean the world is filled with uneducated, foolish readers, nearly blind viewers and tone deaf listeners?

No. It means perfection isn't necessary, and sometimes it is a hindrance. If you want to win an Academy Award for a film you're making, don't expect too many of us outside of the film industry to actually watch it.

Never never never insult the audience.

It's so easy to call out the audience for not being more sophisticated or intelligent, and unable to recognize flawed work, and call "crap" crap. Critics and elitists can say what they want, but ultimately you do want to write something that interests readers if you want to be read.

Instead, consider a lesson from all of this madness. Just because a blog or book is grammatically perfect and the spelling is absolutely correct, without a single solitary typo to be found and it does all the right things in all the right places, that doesn't mean anyone is going to want to read it. As a matter of fact, it might be so by-the-book that the majority of readers will be put off by it.

Humans are *not* perfect, and we know it.

Pop culture is always more popular, not because it sucks and fans just don't get what art really is, but because it seems more "real" and "connected," even if flawed, and people like that. It reminds us of ourselves. If you can give a reader the gift of "themselves," you're on to something. No one really wants to be disconnected. Do they?

Self-Publishing, DOOM!

Some editors, traditional publishers and even writers are going crazy over self-publishing because they think it is destroying industry standards and quality. Disaster, they say! Unmitigated disaster! How soon we forget. Recording artists have been self-publishing their work for decades. Without self-publishing we may have never heard of Elvis, perhaps the most recognized name in music still today.

Elvis Presley (the King, mind you), was discovered because he self-published a song for his mother. Then, when he finally hit the stage, all hell broke loose. He was described as reckless, raw, and unprofessional, and oh, let's not forget, too sexual. He was about as imperfect as they came at the time. "True professional" artists not only insulted Elvis, but because they were insulting him, they indirectly insulted his audience, too. An audience that grew to include most of the world's population.

Those "true professionals" said his voice wasn't good enough, and because of their influence, Presley's break-out hit was delayed until he took it upon himself to sing a cover of "That's All Right" (originally by Arthur Crudup) just after a recording session of standard oh-so-yawn-invoking material. "That's All Right" wasn't intended to be recorded. He apparently just sang it for fun – to be himself.

Elvis sang "That's All Right" his way and it was recorded. Bill Black remarked, "Damn. Get that on the radio and they'll run us out of town." So they put it on the B side of "Blue Moon of Kentucky." Ah, those of little faith. Once the audience heard "That's All Right," they went crazy for it and the rest, as they say, is history. *Love me tender, love me true...*

Here's the thing: as writers we are way (and I mean waaaay) too hard on ourselves. We read too many books on editing, how to write flawlessly and we allow standards from bygone eras to keep us in a box while the rest of the world that "doesn't know any better" moves on. And what does this do? Make us better writers? Not always. Mostly it just serves as food for doubt. "Why doesn't anyone care anymore?" we ask ourselves.

Maybe you're not the next Hemingway, but do you want to be? Seriously? You don't need to be perfect and you don't need to write something critics will love and sing praises for.

Hey, if you're lucky, maybe your writing will create a lynch mob of critics who will write scathing remarks about your work. I hope they do, because if they do then you will have written something that matters! It also means you're attracting an audience. Trust me, critics won't care about you if you do not have an audience, because their job depends on an audience, too.

Why do so many blogs and books fail?

I answered this question, but really, it's not as important as figuring out why popular blogs and books, which seem "flawed," do very well. It's not that complicated. The authors write about what interests them and their audiences, and they aren't all that concerned with the literary police picking them up for a WUI (Writing Under the Influence). They've got something to say that matters and people want to hear it.

Now, I'm not saying you should throw caution to the wind and not make your work presentable. Having your work proofread and cleaned up so that it's not totally annoying to read is still the right thing to do. What I *am* saying is loosen up and stop being so hard on yourself and your writing. Don't let Writer's Doubt take over. No, you really don't want to do that.

Here's my advice. Take a break from reading about how to write better and go write without worrying about perfection and approval. Just write. Let go. It doesn't have to be perfect, but if you let go and write something that matters, it might be good enough. And if it's not? Start over and write some more. Keep going – keep writing. Strive for connection and not perfection.

One Sure-Fire Way to Find Your Passion

By Bryan Hutchinson

A lot of people are finding out that following their passion is fraught with difficulty, pain and suffering, and sometimes it's unbearable. But what if they're mistaken and it's not their passion that they are following?

Whatever your dream is, that's your passion. Right? Not so fast. That's not always the case and if you're someone who has fallen for this trap it could be the reason you are miserably following the wrong path. Then again, maybe you have found your passion. In that case, this post will likely be irrelevant to you. (Unless you're in the trap and merely think you've found your passion.)

Achieving Your Dream

Common wisdom dictates that following your passion is living your dream. But what is your dream? What's so special about it? And finally, what are you willing to struggle through to achieve it? Those are three very important questions, and if you can answer all three of them you may be able to determine if you're following your passion or in the trap. We'll go over the questions together in a moment.

I mistook one of my dreams for my passion.

My favorite hobby is playing pool (billiards). I don't play it as much as I used to and that's okay. When I do get the opportunity to play, I enjoy the sheer fun of hitting the balls around and competing with friends for bragging rights. It wasn't always that way.

When I was about 16 years old I discovered I had a natural talent for playing pool and, with very little actual practice other than playing with some friends, I was soon winning local house tournaments by the age of 17. It was exhilarating and a lot of fun not knowing what I was doing, but doing it exceptionally well.

It's while winning those local tournaments that things changed and the fun got zapped right out of the game I had been growing to love. Winning made me start to have dreams of grandeur of larger, more important tournaments with big cash prizes and big trophies to match. And seasoned players noticed me and began filling my head with the belief that I could make a career of playing pool.

Maybe. (You know there's always a maybe.) If I practiced enough, competed with the best, became fully dedicated, and basically breathed pool day in and day out. I might make it, maybe.

It sounded great and for a while I did exactly what was suggested. I ate, drank and breathed pool, and only after a few short years, I was playing on the Master's tour. It wasn't long before I ranked as high as 3rd overall on the tour. But there was a problem. I loved playing pool and I even loved competing, but what I didn't love was all the time it was taking from my daily life and all of the things I had to give up in order to play at a competitive level. 3rd on the tour with all the recognition that came with it was exhilarating and it's what I thought I wanted, but it wasn't enough. I'd have to get even better if I wanted to turn playing pool into a real career, and in order to do that I'd have to give up even more and more. How far was I willing to go?

How far are you willing to go for a dream?

It's great to have a dream about standing on the podium in glory and lining your pockets with prize money, but that's the dream, the end result. There's another part of the dream, though; it's the part you don't actually enjoy if you're not following your passion. The part I'm talking about is giving up major parts of your life to pursue your dream, spending every waking hour practicing, striving and struggling to get just a little bit better and doing everything and anything that is absolutely necessary to achieve victory. In my dream it was the crowning glory that I had visualized and not the hard work and sacrifices. This is where all the old clichés should be inserted, such as "Buck up!" – "Stick with it." – "Put your nose to the grindstone." And "Don't be a quitter."

I quit.

One day during a league tournament, after my last match, I put my pool cue in its leather case, walked over to our team captain and said "I'm done." Just like that. Really. I never looked back. I was 31 years old and I had spent more than a decade chasing the wrong dream until I finally realized that it wasn't my passion. Living in pool halls the rest of my life wasn't what I wanted, and I wasn't willing to struggle another minute for it.

Friends and fellow players thought I was crazy. Many of them told me I was a fool for wasting my talent, that I was a quitter, and, of course, insisted that if I had just dedicated myself more and worked even harder, I would have "made it." Their taunts remind me of a Rocky movie, urging me to get back in the ring and go for it! But that's the thing...

Passion is not always what movies make it out to be, especially if you're going after the wrong dream. Playing pool and winning major championships is not my passion. It may have been one of my dreams, but it was never my passion. I got caught in the deadly trap of going after the wrong dream.

Why is the trap deadly?

Because of the years of life it can steal from you. Don't get me wrong, I learned many valuable lessons I would not have learned otherwise, and I do believe things happen for a reason. Still, had I considered all of the ramifications of what was involved in becoming a pool champion when I started, I might have reconsidered.

What's your passion?

What I've discovered is this: *Passion is found in the struggles you can't live without.*

I don't agree with the idea that you should struggle through anything and everything simply because of a dream. That is, if your dream is only the crowning glory, e.g. winning a world championship, making partner in a law firm, or publishing a bestselling book, and not the extraordinary effort it takes to achieve it. Passion is when you love doing something for the sake of doing it, regardless of what it may or may not lead to. In pool, I was striving for a result, but what I had to do to get the results I desired was killing me inside.

3 very important questions about your dream:

Most of us dream wonderful dreams of grandeur, and that's okay, but it's imperative to know if the dream you're striving for is your passion or not, and these three questions may help.

1. What is your dream?

Identify it, and if you have more than one, identify them all. It's perfectly okay to dream of becoming an astronaut and being the first person to walk on Mars. That was one of my childhood dreams.

2. What's so special about it?

Consider writing out your answer. If you have more than one dream, write your answer for each one. My dream about becoming an astronaut was special because I'd get to be the first person to walk on Mars.

3. What are you willing to struggle through to achieve it and how far are you willing to go?

This is the most important question, because the answer will help you realize whether a dream is worth pursuing. Let's say you dream of becoming an astronaut. Are you willing to get all the necessary education, join the military, become an elite pilot, go to more school, endure more years of training, and then finally apply to NASA? (I'm sure I'm missing a lot of steps in there, but you get the picture.)

If you answer a resounding, even excited, YES! to all of those questions, then your dream of becoming an astronaut is probably your passion.

In my case, I'm terribly scared of heights and I can barely board a plane without major drugs, for Pete's sake. So no, my dream of walking on Mars was only a dream, not my passion. And what's more important is that I have absolutely no interest in doing all that other stuff I listed above to become an astronaut.

I'm a writer. My passion is *writing*.

I've written page after page for days and weeks, and many I tucked away never to be used or seen again. And, that's okay. I don't mind it one bit. I've published books that have become bestsellers and I've published books that have barely made their money back (some haven't), and that's okay, too.

When it comes to writing, I love the work. I love the misery. I love bleeding on the page. I love overcoming Writer's Doubt. Those are struggles I can't live without. (However, when you're following your true passion, what other people identify as "struggles" might not feel like struggling to you.)

I also love the joy of writing, writing with abandon and the satisfaction of finishing, and then starting all over again.

My dream with regard to writing is to write about my experiences and lessons learned and hopefully help a few people along the way. I'm not the best writer in the world, far from it, and I don't have any desire to become the best, but I look forward to waking up each morning and working at improving every day for the rest of my life.

That, at least to me, is true passion. Doing what I do no matter what the challenges are, or how much I have to struggle, or how heart wrenching it is to be rejected and criticized, and even if there is not a single scratch of gold at the end of the rainbow. I love it anyway.

When you love the process of whatever you do, the good – the bad and the ugly of it – *that's* when you've found your passion.

Use Discipline to Cultivate the Creative Flow

By Stacy Claflin of *StacyClaflin.com*

Discipline vs Creativity OR Discipline and Creativity?

Discipline is often thought to be the opposite of creativity. The reality, however, is that the right kinds of discipline can help spur on creativity in new and exciting ways.

Often, I speak with aspiring authors and one thing that many of them have in common is that they tend to wait until inspiration hits before they sit down to write. They want the internal muse to start singing and dancing before they create the art. I'm not speaking poorly of anyone. I remember going through that phase myself.

I also talk with lot of published authors, some of whom are extremely successful, and I can't think of a single one who waits for a wave of inspiration.

What do the published authors have in common?

Schedule

They all have a set writing schedule that they adhere to. They have either found the time that best fits their schedule or they make their schedule fit around their best time of day to write. However they do it, they make sure that it happens.

Creating art doesn't just happen.

In my case, the best time for me to write is when everyone else is sleeping. It's dark, it's quiet, and I'm able to work without interruption. So I write between the hours of 4-6 a.m. And no, I'm not a morning person. But I've trained myself to wake up early and start writing. The first thing that I started doing was setting my alarm five minutes earlier each day. The thrill of writing so many words each day keeps me getting up early six days a week.

Success inspires more success.

Preparation

Published authors prepare before writing. No matter what type of art you create, you must prepare yourself. If you're going to throw a pot on a wheel, you don't sit down at the wheel hoping that clay will hop on and form into a vessel. You first need to prepare the wheel, grab some clay, throw on an apron, and plan out what you're going to make.

Writing is the same way. Even the most talented writer who sits down in front of blank page (or screen) will have trouble typing out words with no groundwork laid.

Plotting

The authors who write the most words per day swear by plotting—outlining, writing story beats, or whatever you want to call it. My personal method, which has me writing 1,000 words per half hour at my fastest to date, is to write a very rough outline for the entire novel before I write a single word.

Then each day, when I'm done with my daily writing, I jot down a couple paragraphs about what I need to write during my next writing session. In my case, a couple of paragraphs is more than enough for me get out 2,000 words. The process is different for everyone. Some writers outline one sentence per every hundred words they write.

It doesn't matter how you do it, as long as you figure out what works best for you.

Education

Learning about your craft is important. Why reinvent the wheel when you don't have to? I don't want to reinvent anything! I want to spend my time creating. It's an exciting time that we live in: Information is at our fingertips, and it takes little to no effort or cost to learn something new every day.

Message Boards or Groups

Joining a group of your peers – or those who are where you want to be – is a wonderful way to increase your knowledge! Do a Google search for message boards on your topic of interest or search for Facebook groups. Use your imagination and soon you'll be sitting at the feet of people who are making a living at what you dream of doing.

Blogs

Do you know how many experts and professionals give away information on a daily basis? A lot of them! Start searching or asking around and follow some prominent bloggers. Get their email notifications and follow their advice.

Podcasts

Another great way to learn about becoming more productive in your creativity is to listen to podcasts. Reading words on the screen is not the only way to learn. We all learn through more than one of our senses, so hearing about your craft can make a deeper impact on what you learn.

You can also learn in different settings. I love listening to podcasts while I'm in the fresh air, throwing the ball for my dog. Being outside opens up our senses and can help us learn more easily. If I worked outside the home, I know that I would use my commute time for listening to podcasts. Be creative – that's the point, isn't it?

Online Courses

If you've been to college, you know how expensive education can be. I graduated over a decade ago and I'm still paying off those debts. An online course is nowhere near the cost, and you can learn so much from them. If you're a writer, I highly recommend Tribe Writers and Story Cartel. (Visit the writing resources link provided at the end of this book for more details about these courses.)

Shattering the Myths about the Midas Touch and Success

By Bryan Hutchinson

There's a common belief that we need the Midas touch to become a bestselling author like Stephen King, a famous TV host like Oprah, or even a successful producer like David Geffen.

But do we, really?

Today I'm going to shatter myths about the Midas touch and share with you what we all do have within us that is much, much better.

The Midas Touch

The phrase "the Midas touch" comes from the Greek myth about King Midas for his ability to turn everything he touched to gold. Today it is often used to describe people who seem to always do extraordinary well.

If we don't have the Midas touch, so the thinking goes, then it's not our fault if we don't succeed.

First, the word "fault" needs to be banished because it implies you weren't born to succeed, and second, it's just not true! You were born to be the best you can be, and that, my friends, is more than good enough. I used to believe in the Midas touch. Not exactly by that name, though. I'm not sure what I called it, but the idea was clear to me. I wasn't good enough. I didn't have what it takes.

Maybe you believed in it, too? The problem is that such a belief only serves to limit us, so it is important to step back and put it into perspective.

Midas Touch Myth #1

Highly successful people had it easier. There could be nothing further from the truth. Actually, when you research famous, successful people, you will discover that a great many of them have been in horrific situations and come from less than ideal backgrounds. Consider David Geffen who signed Bob Dylan and Crosby, Stills and Nash and was a founding member of DreamWorks. But, as a young man David was extremely poor and his bed was the family's couch in their one-bedroom apartment. Fortunately, David was able to go to college, but he flunked out. Today David Geffen is a billionaire, and not because he was born into money or had it any easier than others. He found his passion and lives it to the fullest.

Midas Touch Myth #2

Highly successful people never miss goals, make mistakes, get rejected or fail at anything.

The reality is that we all miss goals and we all fail at one time or another. That's life, and those who seem to be blessed with success miss goals and fail too, Sometimes they crash and burn so bad it takes them years to recover. But that's the key; they keep going, even after they could have given up. It's about learning from your mistakes, overcoming the most difficult challenges and persevering through adversity.

One of the reasons this myth is so predominant is that people who succeed come into our consciousness only after they've overcome their struggles. The public in general has no clue what the person went through or overcame challenges.

Three Hundred Million

Not only was Stephen King rejected dozens of times, one publisher went so far as to say this: "We are not interested in science fiction which deals with negative utopias. They do not sell." How would a rejection letter like that make you feel? As you well know, Stephen didn't stop writing science fiction which deals with negative utopias, and he's sold over 350 million copies of his books so far!

Midas Touch Myth #3

People who make it and achieve great success are naturally happy and positive and never get down on themselves. They've always had the good life. It's true that attitude plays a major role in any kind of success, be it in writing, in business and even in relationships. However, maintaining a positive attitude is something we must work at every day. That goes for everyone, even the most positive, happy person you know.

Consider Oprah: she was repeatedly abused as a child in the most despicable way. Wouldn't you agree that she has every right to be angry and cynical? And yet, those things do not define her. She found her way, and even though she lives with memories of her past, she chooses to find positive ways to help others, and ultimately, to be happy despite the pain she endured.

It's far easier to be cynical and negative. We all know that. We've all been down on ourselves and we've all felt the pain of failing and the sorrow of loss. It's what we do in spite of those things that makes the difference.

Don't fall for the myths No, don't do it. It's not worth it. One day you may be the next success story to show up on a popular TV talk show, and many viewers will believe you got lucky, or you had some kind of advantage, or you were perfectly unrejectable and, of course, you never made any mistakes. None. Because you're obviously perfect.

But you'll know the truth.

How to Become a Prolific Writer While Holding Down a Day Job

By Bryan Hutchinson

One of the most frequent questions I receive is: How can I write and hold down a day job at the same time?

There's a common belief (and a few myths that support it) that you can only do one or the other. But that's not true.

I have a day job, and I enjoy it. I also enjoy writing and publishing. Maybe you're kind of stuck in a place where I once was and you're only writing when you feel inspired and can fit it in here and there. I figured out that if I wanted to be a writer who actually writes and publishes, I needed to take my writing seriously and give it the time and consideration it deserves.

It hasn't always been easy and there have been times it just hasn't worked out, but for the most part I've succeeded in holding down a 40+ hour week job, authoring a dozen books, and maintaining several blogs, not to mention writing magazine and newspaper articles.

I don't share this with you to boast. No. It's been too exhausting at times for that, but it is to say...

It can be done.

Yes, it's been exhausting at times, but it has also been incredibly rewarding. Day jobs last until you quit or retire, but a writing career can last your entire life, and the writing itself can last for infinity.

Myths about Writing and Working

To make debunking the following myths fun, I'll use examples from the writing lives of well-known authors:

Myth: If you have a day job you can't be an author.

Debunk: The author of *Alice's Adventures in Wonderland*, Lewis Carroll (real name, Charles Lutwidge Dodgson), continued to work day jobs throughout his life. With growing wealth and fame, Carroll continued to teach at Christ Church until 1881 and remained in residence there until his death. He was also a working mathematician of note and a photographer.

Other authors who held down day jobs throughout their writing careers include Bram Stoker, Philip Larkin, T.S. Eliot, and Virginia Woolf, among many others.

Myth: You can't write a bestselling book and work a day job at the same time.

Debunk: I present you with none other than Anne Rice. Rice has held a variety of jobs, including waitress, cook, and theater usherette, among others. In fact, she wrote the bestselling book *Interview with the Vampire* while working her day job as an insurance claims examiner.

Myth: A day job kills your inspiration and motivation to write.

Debunk: A day job can be a great source of inspiration and motivation for writing. In fact, who knows? It could provide you with inspiration and motivation to create change and hope in the world.

John Green intended to become an Episcopal priest, but his experiences of working in a hospital with children suffering from life-threatening illnesses inspired him to become an author, and later to write *The Fault in Our Stars*.

Maintain daily writing rituals

In my book *Writer's Doubt*, I discuss the importance of daily writing rituals in order to write every day consistently. The gist of it is: Repeat the same actions daily to create a habit for writing at a specific time and place every day.

If you examine your daily routines, you'll discover things you do on a regular basis and in a specific order. And that's a good thing. What you want to do is fit your writing into your daily routine and allow it to become one of your habits.

For example, every morning you wake up and do things in a certain way. Perhaps you first make coffee, then breakfast, then brush your teeth, etc...

Having a day job makes it imperative that I allocate time for writing. I insure I write at least 2 hours before I go to work, come rain or shine. And I do this by following my rituals every morning without fail. Regardless of what time I work (shift work), I wake up at least 3 hours prior, and like clockwork, 1) I brush my teeth, 2) make breakfast, 3) sit down at my desk, 4) check emails, 5) check in on my social connections, and finally 5) after stretching my legs for a moment, I write on cue for at least two hours. (Parents I know who write and work day jobs tend to pick times to write before their children wakeup or after they go to bed.)

Whether my writing is good, bad, or ugly is irrelevant.

I write a minimum of 500 words each day thanks to my daily writing rituals. Mind you, I'm not writing every day because I'm especially motivated or inspired. I'm writing because I made it a habit for me to start writing at a certain time and place every morning.

How to make writing part of your daily routine:

---

1. Take note of the things you do consistently every day before and after work. Consider writing them down so you can become more conscious of them.

2. Create a space of time within your current daily rituals for writing every day. Make sure it's at a time of day that works best for you. I write best in the morning and other people write better at night. When do you write best?

3. Commit. It's important to commit to writing at the same time every day so that it becomes a natural, automatic part of your day, regardless of whether you feel inspired or motivated. It's believed that it takes 21 days to create a habit, so hang in there and keep going. In my personal experience it takes up to 60 to 90 days, but I'm stubborn like that.

Sacrifice

Yes, like it or not, when we commit to writing every day, sacrifices (choices) will have to be made. Many of us have hobbies that we do every day, such as playing tennis, or golf, or running, or going to the gym. What will you give up or cut back on? Unfortunately, we don't have unlimited hours in a day – only 24.

Maybe it's your writing that you're already sacrificing for something else? Be honest.

I used to play in a pool league and I needed to practice at least 2 hours a day to stay competitive at the level I was at. When I decided to take my writing seriously, I needed to eliminate an hour of pool practice a day, and eventually, as I wrote more and more, I stopped playing pool in the league. That was my choice, my sacrifice, as it were.

I sacrificed pool for writing, but I had been sacrificing my writing for pool. Maybe you don't have to sacrifice anything for the craft, but do keep in mind that the more you do the less time you have for each and that means you'll be giving less of yourself to something. You decide what deserves your time and focus. So decide.

Writing Sanctuary

I've found it extremely helpful to have a writing sanctuary in my home, a place where I feel comfortable and everything I need is within reach. This place for me happens to be my writing desk in my office. It is free of clutter, with only a notepad and a few pens and pencils, my keyboard and my computer monitor. Oh, and a coaster for my cup of coffee. I can't write without my coffee.

I highly recommend creating a writing sanctuary for yourself, somewhere you only go to write, and therefore, your mind will associate being there with writing.

Once I'm in my sanctuary I'm ready in mind, body and soul for the business of writing, and I write.

It's about writing

Ultimately, becoming a prolific writer is about writing. Incorporating the craft into my daily rituals and making it a habit (like, say, breathing) has worked wonders for me. I hope it works wonders for you, too.

Starting Over Is Essential to Your Creativity and Success

By Bryan Hutchinson

Have you ever been ready to throw your work in the air and give up? Who hasn't? Hey, maybe starting over isn't such a bad idea.

Yesterday I was talking with a friend over coffee when he told me he doesn't get it. "What don't you get?" I asked him. He explained that every time he starts a creative project, writing a book in this case, he comes to a point where he realizes he must start over because it's just not good enough or doesn't make any sense.

As he was explaining his face took on an exhausted and frustrated look. I recognized it instantly, because I've seen it so many times... in the mirror. My friend was suffering from a common issue that most all of us go through when we find ourselves starting over. We tend to think it indicates our work isn't good enough or that we have somehow failed, but the reality is that starting over isn't about either of those things.

It's not anyone's fault that we see it this way, because over the last hundred years the industrialized world has become all about standards and measurements, with little to no patience for the creative process. In fact, until the previous decade, creativity had been practically removed from most people's lives.

"Do it right the first time" became the mantra, and standards were put in place to insure you did do it right the first time. But now that the world is once again changing; more and more people are going back to their creative roots, and the process of creativity must be rediscovered.

It's kind of scary, I know. But it's okay. It's okay to start over. We'd all like to start a project and see it to fruition in one go, but the reality is we need to start over. The human mind is designed to contemplate, to learn, to grow and to seek out and find solutions and new ideas.

Whenever we begin a new creative project, it's usually from a vague idea, a mere inkling of what we really want and it takes working it to discover if an idea has any potential to blossom. The first draft may seem like a garbled mess, but it's really the way the brain works through thoughts and ideas. Our brains work this way all the time without us taking conscious notice of it.

Quiet your mind and try to follow your thoughts, and you'll discover they seem scattered and random. That's why meditation can be so difficult. As creatives, we are fortunate (or unfortunate, you pick) to see our confusing thoughts in writing or on a canvas, and it can be disturbing.

When you start a creative endeavor, be it writing a book, painting a picture, or sculpting a portrait, it's absolutely natural to start over, putting aside the first effort, and second, or even the third until the right words, the right colors, or the right shapes finally come to you. This is why we are taught that it is better to let go when writing the first draft, because when you try to control and edit it, you're disturbing your brain's natural process, and as a result you become frustrated.

We must go to the edge of quitting.

It's happened to me many times after writing several drafts that when I am about ready to quit and throw my keyboard into the trash, the idea suddenly begins to take shape in a coherent form. When this happens, my writing becomes like a symphony and the angels sing. I often wondered in exasperation why I always seem to go to the very edge of quitting before I start writing something that makes sense. Because that's the way the brain works.

We might not understand how our brains are putting ideas and thoughts together to form our concept, but we do know it feels exhausting and it's hard to trust that somehow it will put everything together to create something that matters.

Each time we start over, or begin a new draft, the message becomes clearer and it is the process of starting over that makes this possible.

Consider Thomas Edison – why is he famous? Is Edison more famous for his inventions or for how many times he started over and did not give up? Thomas Edison's story is so inspiring and motivating because it tells the truth of human nature about how we learn and grow, and ultimately, hopefully, succeed.

We make mistakes (or we call them mistakes) and we start over, but without doing so success would not be possible. The next time you start a project, try not to worry too much about whether it will unfold perfectly or not. Just know that you are on the right track you if you feel compelled to start over again.

"Many of life's failures are experienced by people who did not realize how close they were to success when they gave up." –Thomas Edison

Don't give up.

It's okay to become frustrated and exhausted. Go for a walk or get a drink of water, and then start again.

Never throw away any of your drafts. They may seem like a mess, but if you wait a few days and read them again, you are likely to find a few gems, a delightful word here and a beautiful sentence there, and you may discover the writing is not as incoherent as you thought.

Here's the thing: you're never really starting over; you're simply taking the next step in the creative process. So go ahead. Take the next step.

Why No One is Paying Attention to You (and How to Change It)

By Bryan Hutchinson

Everyone wants to know how to get more attention for their work, but not everyone is willing to do what it takes. The question you have to ask yourself is a simple one, and yet it's profound and can change everything. Are you willing to do what it takes?

If yes, continue. If no, then stop reading now.

What follows is some tough love, but if you are serious about getting attention, then you'll want to read this. Not all of what I listed below will apply to you, but if one or two do, then you'll have something tangible to consider and work on – if you choose to.

1. You Haven't Admitted You Want Attention

Most people fail to gain attention because they are not willing to admit to themselves that they want it, or at one time or another they did admit it, but then gave up too soon.

"I'm a writer. That's what I do. People should read my work because I write and if they don't read it, I don't care." Those would be famous last words if anyone read them, but the writers who wrote them never got enough attention for anyone to read them, much less care. Only when you admit you truly want it will you be willing to do the work necessary to gain it.

2. You're Not Willing to Do the Work

Oh, you're willing to write, paint, or sculpt, but are you willing to do the work it takes to gain the attention you want? Are you willing to investigate what it takes and work hard at it day in and day out?

Writing, painting and sculpting are not enough unless you are the next Van Gogh, but then again that might not be true since he died poor and in obscurity. Van Gogh had a good excuse; in his time there was no internet and no way to instantly share his work with the world. You live in a time when it is possible to reach millions by publishing online, and yet millions of people publish every day and still don't capture much attention. This doesn't mean they haven't written or drawn masterpieces. What this means is that there is more work to be done.

You have to reach out, join communities and become a valuable member within your niche. You have to consistently work hard to get people interested and work even harder to keep them interested.

3. It's All about You

Attention is the currency of online traffic and like any other currency, you have to earn it. It's not all about you, and not everyone cares about what you care about. As a writer, you must make what you write about interesting to others by finding fresh and exciting ways to write about it. Stay up to date with the latest news in your niche, give your unbiased opinion and offer useful advice unique to your experiences.

Online currency may be attention, but the true gold is generosity. Most aren't willing to be very generous, so give your all. Those who are too busy trying to take attention will never truly gain it.

4. Not Determined to Make a Difference

You can't be tentative or unsure. You have to be clear about who you are, what you are writing about and establish yourself as someone who can be trusted. You absolutely must be ready and willing to make a difference. We (the audience) don't want to hear from anyone who is not willing to stand for something. If you're not out to make a difference, then we don't have time for you. If you think about it, you don't really have time for anyone who is peddling what you have already read, seen or heard a hundred times before.

Be unique, stand for something, and make a difference.

5. You Deserve Attention

No, you don't. Not if you're not willing to do the work and create the art it takes to capture and hold our attention. If we are not worth the effort and consideration, then you DO NOT deserve our attention. That's the hardest truth for most of us to accept. Accept it and then do something about it. And know this; no matter what your inner critic tells you, you DO have what it takes.

"The greater danger for most of us lies not in setting our aim too high and falling short; but in setting our aim too low, and achieving our mark." –Michelangelo

6. You're Too Worried about Criticism

Aren't we all? If you create work that matters and share it, you will attract critics. You will not become a recognized artist until you have a few haters. Don't hide from them, because if you do you'll end up hiding from the rest of us, too.

When the hate mail, angry comments and spiteful reviews start coming in remember to laugh about them, because they are giving you acknowledgement that your work mattered enough for them to comment. After all, how often do you comment on something that just doesn't matter?

The more critics you have, the better. You might not think so right now, but consider what happens when you hide and avoid critics by holding your best work back. What then? There's one word for it: Obscurity.

7. You Are Riddled with Doubt

All artists are riddled with doubt. Know this: the more you doubt yourself and your art, the closer you are to creating work that matters. You are on the threshold. Now it's time to make a choice. Are you going to let that pesky critical voice within you win, or are you going to ship? No one can simply decide to overcome doubt, and "poof!" it will be gone. No. But if you're willing to admit doubt is holding you back, then you can begin to find and use strategies to loosen its grip and take control of your destiny as an artist.

What You CAN Do Now

It's time to make a difference and get noticed. You can, if you choose to. When you decide to make a difference and you're willing to be generous enough to share your work with us and to do what it takes to let us know you exist in this world, then and only then will we pay attention to you. Not before.

It's not easy to gain attention. It's hard work: it takes determination and it takes time. Every "overnight success" has more work behind them doing more tedious stuff than they get credit for. Many have tried before you, and many have given up telling themselves they don't need it or want it.

There's nothing wrong with creating art only for yourself, but please don't fool yourself into believing you are not good enough to gain our attention. The next time you feel like giving up, remember it means you are close to the threshold. Are you going to keep moving forward or are you going to stall? Don't stop. Keep going.

That's the only way you will ever gain our attention. Sooner or later it will be your turn, but only if you embrace the challenges and keep on keeping on.

7 Inspirational Quotes that Could Change Your Life

By Bryan Hutchinson

Every now and then you read a book, watch a movie or simply hear a story where you learn something that dramatically changes your life. It's profound when it happens. But as remarkable as it may be, it is also rare and unpredictable. I've come to realize such special lessons only come when the moment is right. Call it destiny if you will, but I believe when the student is ready, the master will appear. I also believe we will not move on to the next lesson until we've fully understood, accepted and embraced the last one. Today, I'd like to share the most powerful lessons I have learned.

Here are 7 quotes that encompass lessons that have changed my life and maybe they'll change yours, too:

"Believe in yourself. Have faith in your abilities. Without a humble but reasonable confidence in your own powers you cannot be successful or happy." —Norman Vincent Peale

Peale's quote encompasses the message of his book *The Power of Positive Thinking*. A friend loaned me his copy of this book, and from the very first page I became enthralled. I knew I could improve and become a better person, but never understood how, and *The Power of Positive Thinking* taught me how. I can never fully explain how life-changing Peale's book was for me. The lessons contained in it started me on a new journey, one that is positive and hopeful. I learned to embrace every day with a humble but reasonable confidence in myself and my abilities.

I highly recommend *The Power of Positive Thinking* to anyone, especially if you have been struggling for some time, and you want to find a way to rise above your struggles.

"If you don't design your own life plan, chances are you'll fall into someone else's plan. And guess what they have planned for you? Not much." —Jim Rohn

Few teachers teach lessons that are so direct, honest and significant. Rohn often talked about possibilities and opportunities as wind and how the wind blows around all of us, but the difference is how you set your sail.

Peale's lesson came first and I am fortunate it did. Had I not learned the lessons of positive thinking, I would not have been ready to design my own life plan. I would not have written my memoir and self-published it.

By writing, self-publishing, and even starting my blogs, I began to design my own life as a writer. I could have continued to write in my personal journals and stayed in obscurity, but that would have been self-limiting.

So what's your passion? Have you designed your own plan to bring life to your passion? If you're waiting for someone else to give you an opportunity or to design your life plan for you, well, be prepared if they don't have much in store for you.

Go ahead, set your own sail.

"Don't let what you can't do stop you from doing what you can do." —John Wooden

Oh boy, one of the most important lessons of all. Our failures, our mistakes and our weaknesses are usually at the forefront of our minds. It's natural and normal to want to improve in the things we do not do well, but our energy would be better spent focusing on the things we do well. Don't let what you can't do hold you back from doing what you can do.

In other words, set your sail by your strengths. Embrace your passion and allow your strengths to grow. Your confidence in your abilities will naturally grow as well.

"Anyone who has never made a mistake has never tried anything new." —Albert Einstein

We all make mistakes, plain and simple. Some mistakes are major, but most are minor and repairable. However, the only way to avoid a mistake is to attempt nothing at all. Is that really an option? I used to fear making mistakes. I always took the path of least resistance, so I thought. It's better to do what you want to do and learn from the mistakes you make. You're going to make them, but you may discover they are not so bad after all. Whenever you learn from a mistake, you improve and grow from it. Well, my friends, there's a great sense of accomplishment and satisfaction in that.

"Half the failures in life arise from pulling in the horse as he is leaping." —Augustus William Hare and Julius Charles Hare

Too many people have given up just when they were about to cross the finish line. The problem was they didn't know they were so close. If you're going to do something, be prepared to go all the way. Fear and doubt will always find their way into our consciousness when we attempt to go beyond what we've done before, and if we let them, they will stop us. The key is to follow through all the way to the finish. We usually come up short because we stop ourselves when it gets too tough and seems hopeless. On the contrary, that's when you're about to make a breakthrough.

Keep going. Be all in.

"You have to let people see what you wrote. It will never be perfect, but perfect is overrated." —Tina Fey

Perfection is unachievable and irrelevant and yet too many of us get caught up trying to achieve it. Do what you can to the best of your ability. You'll discover that most of the time, that's good enough.

"If today were the last day of my life, would I want to do what I am about to do today?" —Steve Jobs

One of the most valuable lessons in life is learning to enjoy each day, each moment and do what you are about to do with purpose. Simply going through the motions is not enough. You've got to be intentional about your life. Are you happy? Are you doing what you want to be doing? If so, that's fantastic. If not, then what are you going to do today?

How to Achieve Greatness as a Writer

By Bryan Hutchinson

Do you ever get the feeling that you're spinning your wheels? You know you are doing your best, but still it feels as though you are only going through the motions. Perhaps what you actually feel is you are not doing what you were meant to do. For whatever reason it seems like you're not making any progress; you've reached a plateau and that's it.

It's a letdown, because you know deep down that you could be doing so much better. You were meant for more. You were meant for greatness. You have a special feeling inside of you. It's a feeling that compels you to continue even when you believe all is lost, that your moment has passed and there's no reason to continue striving.

But you do. You continue.

You do not continue because anyone tells you to, although some have. No – you continue because you can't help it. No matter how many times you quit, no matter how many times you give up, something makes you try again.

It's true. You know it is.

Indeed, you have a very special feeling inside of you. But if you're honest, this special feeling scares you a little. It tugs, it pulls, it beckons, and it scares you, because it indicates you are not living entirely up to your potential, and each day that goes by is another day you didn't reach your destiny.

For many, destiny is considered a dangerous belief because it's a mythical destination far, far away and there is no roadmap to get there. Maybe it doesn't exist at all.

What if I told you there is a yellow brick road?

There is. But the first thing you've got to do is stop being so hard on yourself. I don't mean hard on yourself in the sense you shouldn't strive to improve or not to stretch further than you ever have before. No. I am talking about that other hard-on-yourself.

Think about it.

Yes. That one.

As humans we have the terrible habit of putting ourselves down and chastising ourselves for not achieving or accomplishing this or that, even if we don't know exactly what it is we should be doing.

We beat ourselves up day in and day out, instead of realizing that we are on a wonderful journey, a journey we are privileged to be traveling.

Tomorrow is another day. Think about tomorrow.

Think about all the things you can do tomorrow, such as start a new book or prep a new canvas or maybe just go for a walk and enjoy the word's natural art all around you.

What if you didn't have tomorrow to look forward to?

Just for a day, just one, try not to be so hard on yourself and give yourself credit for the work you already do.

Practice gratefulness simply for being here, for the ability to still wield a pen.

Your destiny awaits you, so follow your passion and you will get there. The way to follow your passion is to listen to the special feeling you have inside of you. It's there, and if you remove your fears for only a moment, you will hear it loud and clear.

Listen. Listen closely. Don't block it, ignore it, or tell yourself you're not good enough, because you are. It will help if you realize how precious the journey is.

No matter how hard things have been, no matter the obstacles, the doubts or the fears, open yourself up to realizing that each and every day is a gift. What if there really were no tomorrows?

Live today to its fullest, do the best you can and be kind to yourself.

The special feeling inside that I mentioned? It's special because it lets you know that you are meant for greatness. Not for riches or fame, although those may come.

You are meant for greatness.

Greatness is living today to its fullest, doing the very best we can, and when we lay our heads down to rest, we might whisper: *I am thankful for today. I wasn't perfect, but I did my best. Today was a good day and tomorrow will be even better.*

You will rock the world.

We all have the desire to do something special, to create art that will rock the world. You can, and you will. But you'll have to let down your guard and be kind to yourself, grateful for what you already have and what you are already doing.

My advice is to treasure each day you're privileged to have and do the best you can in the time you've been given. Don't rush, and don't give in to your doubts and fears. Do your best every day and you will create your best work. I promise. Follow the yellow brick road:

- Be in the moment. Take notice of today, all aspects of it. Take the pressure off of getting something or somewhere and enjoy the journey.
- Take nothing for granted. Everything happens for a reason.
- Practice gratefulness simply for being you. You are meant to be you. Whatever you create can only come from you, and there was never a better you than who you are right now.
- Use affirmations to condition your mind and remind yourself that you are good enough. You are doing work that matters.
- You are greatness. Accept this truth.

There have been times I have been so hard on myself that I wasted days, weeks, months, and even years, reprimanding myself for not being good enough. The thing is, being hard on ourselves is natural and normal, and most of us were taught that being uncompromising and hard is the only way to be successful.

But really, all we are doing is building more pressure which leads to frustration, anxiety and creating work we are not (and cannot) be happy with. And frankly, when consumed with so much pressure, the journey becomes dispassionate and empty.

It doesn't have to be that way. Remove a little pressure today, a little more tomorrow and eventually you'll be where you want to be, living life to its fullest by enjoying it and living in the moment. If you're in a rush, the quicker way is to help others through their fears, doubts and difficulties. I won't explain why, because if you do it you'll find out soon enough. One word: Magical.

Go ahead and be great, because you already are. Rock the world. And by the way: Your destiny is already here. You're in it. It's called: *Today*.

How to Be Loved for the Work You Love to Do

By Dana Sitar of *Writers Bucket List*

I recently realized what it really means to love the work you do. I've been dragged out of my comfort zone for the first time in a while and forced to run my writing business on the bare minimum — which, beautifully, means everything falls by the wayside while the actual writing comes starkly back into focus.

It's an enlightening feeling to realize you're doing exactly what you're meant to do; your path becomes a little clearer, and the weight of things like stress and exhaustion that we tend to associate with "work" is lifted from your shoulders.

You're awash in honest-to-goodness happiness – an all too rare feeling.

Since leaving my old life and day job about two and a half years ago to pursue some unknown "career in writing", I've written and read a lot about "doing work you love".

The concept is totally en vogue with Millenials, as the internet has helped us realize the world really is our oyster, and we don't have to follow any typical path to career success. We can let our freak flags fly, embrace the artists within, be our own bosses, live the life we want.

You read these inspiring posts from someone who has found her path, who is doing work she loves, who isn't bowing to the system; and you think, "Perhaps I ought to do that, too."

People are throwing off the shackles and pursuing the creative life every day. Then, on the flip side, every day someone throws in the towel and admits she can't hack it, can't take the pressures of entrepreneurship, can't deal with the industry; and she slinks back to a cubicle, a uniform, and a boss.

As it turns out, to "do work you love" is just as easy as we all make it out to be. To be loved for the work you do, however, is a much trickier pursuit. Unfortunately, the latter is what you need to be successful in a creative career.

You finally make the leap to do the work you love; you'll make a living writing, painting, skiing, sculpting, teaching, coaching, whatever. You read all the latest self-help books and blogs, and you take all the right steps to launch into the industry.

You start to share your beautiful work.

And no one cares. No one is paying attention, or worse: They are paying attention, and they don't like what you're selling. They don't understand why this is important to you, or why it should matter in the least to them.

Once you've taken all those steps to forge your path in creative work, you've got to take the steps to find the people who will love it as much as you do. That's really hard. It's not about learning sales tactics to convince them to buy it. It's not about learning networking skills to convince them to support it. It's certainly not about learning the latest SEO tricks to help them Google it.

Being loved for the work you do is all about clarifying your message and understanding your audience. To connect with the people who will love the work you love to create, stop thinking about how to sell the book, blog, service, or widget that promotes your message. Start focusing on the message you want to share and the people you want to share it with.

When you understand who your audience is and why they should listen to you, you'll be able to connect with them and connect them to your work. You'll be able to let go of the pressures of entrepreneurship and focus on why you chose a creative career in the first place: to create.

How do you understand your audience? Just talk to them. It's really as simple as that.

Turn all of the "marketing" tools — social media, blogging, email — into avenues to actually talk to your audience, instead of selling to them. This way, you'll be able to genuinely connect with the people who will love your work — and, in turn, to find that enlightening happiness you keep reading about.

Invaluable Advice from Seth Godin Every Writer Needs to Read

By Bryan Hutchinson

Writers the world over have suffered through unbearable self-doubt, and many have overcome it long enough to write words that matter. But some haven't. And some believe they never will. It doesn't have to be that way.

Too many writers have given in to doubt and have given up the dream of writing their story, and yet they, too, can overcome doubt to write words that matter. The challenge of doubt isn't something you face just once or twice; it's a lifelong struggle. You can't just endure it and let it control your writing future. *You* must take control of it if you want to be a writer who writes.

You must find the will and the way to *diminish doubt*.

We all want to put pen to paper and create, and each morning we wake up with the goal to do just that, but all too often we stop ourselves before we even start. And unfortunately, if you're anything like I was, you're not sure what you can do about it.

Ah, but I am sure if you think about it a little, you'll realize that that's what makes our craft so special, because not just anyone can do it. Not just anyone can wield the power of the pen. It takes courage and boldness, an *audacity* that you were born with.

In truth, there's a lot more we can do about doubt than most of us realize.

You're a writer. You were always meant to be a writer. You know that. But that knowledge, that affirmation, that commitment: it's not always enough. Is it? It's helpful to know in your heart of hearts that you were always meant to write, but it's not always enough.

And worse, sometimes you wonder if it's true. You wonder if you really were born to write. So you ask yourself questions, such as:

Was I truly meant to be a writer?

Am I lying to myself?

Is my heart of hearts being honest with me or just telling me what I want to believe?

And down you go. You spiral out of control.

It doesn't have to be that way.

Writer's Doubt

That's why I wrote *Writer's Doubt*. But who am I to write a book about overcoming the doubt writers have? I'm no Stephen King, Ernest Hemingway, or Seth Godin. I'm no one famous. I've never been on the New York Times Bestseller list. And perhaps I never will be... Just who the hell do I think I am?

That's doubt talking. It's so easy to fall into doubt's trap and believe our words don't matter.

Your. Words. Matter.

They do. Don't they? Of course.

Right?

The Project Killer

A good friend recently sent me a quote by Seth Godin from one of his latest blog posts:

"Doubt is the project killer, and investing in diminishing that doubt is time well spent." –Seth Godin

Seth's words are an important reminder to all writers that we - as creatives, as artisans, as people - we must spend time diminishing our doubts. If we don't, doubt can and will stop us.

Doubt *is* the project killer.

Every writer needs to know this because too often we stop and blame everything else, from the weather to the position of the moon, even our muse (where did she go?), everything and anything except the real culprit. Doubt. Writer's Doubt.

Once identified, doubt **can be** overcome.

Make no mistake, writing is hard work, and overcoming doubt, even diminishing it, is even harder work. It's a job that's never done. But it's worth it.

Any love affair is work, and if you love your craft, then you've got what it takes.

Repeat after me:

I'm a writer. I write. – I start. I finish. And I publish.

That's what writers do. You're audacious like that.

Now go. Get back to work and write words that matters. We need them. We need *your* words.

Just the Beginning

Thank you for reading this collection of blog articles. I'd love for you stop by *Positive Writer* and say hello. It would be great to hear from you. We hold regular writing contests, drawings, giveaways, and other events, so be sure to subscribe to the blog to stay up to date. And don't forget to download your free eBook, *Good Enough*, by going to: http://positivewriter.com/free-ebook-good-enough/

Writing resources: Visit the *Positive Writer* resources for writers: http://positivewriter.com/writing-resources/

Contributors

Joe Bunting is the founder of the www.WritePractice.com. He loves the sound of a good sentence and would like to think of himself as a literary snob but can be kept up far too late by a page turner meant for thirteen-year-old girls. He would like for you not to know that though. He lives with his wife and son outside of Atlanta.

C. S. Lakin is a multi-published bestselling novelist and writing coach. She works full-time as a copyeditor and critiques about two hundred manuscripts a year. She teaches writing workshops and gives instruction on her award-winning blog www.LiveWriteThrive.com. Her book—*The 12 Key Pillars of Novel Construction*—is designed to help writers learn the secrets of cinematic technique.

Shanan Haislip is a full-time business writer, an essayist, and webmaster at www.TheProcrastiwriter.com, a blog about ways to fit writing in around a full-time life (without going insane).

Dana Sitar is an author, blogger, and person living in Wisconsin. She writes about writing, life, and love for blogs and books and sometimes things people care about, like *Huffington Post* and that time she had an article published in *The Onion*. Dana shares resources, tips, and tools for writers in search of a path at www.WritersBucketList.com.

Bryan Collins is a writer, blogger and copywriter and the author of a *Handbook for the Productive Writer*. In another life, he worked as a journalist and a radio producer. Before that, he plucked chickens. Bryan is passionate about helping people accomplish more with their writing projects, and when he's not writing, he's running. He lives an hour outside of Dublin. Visit Bryan at www.BecomeaWriterToday.com.

Liwen Y. Ho works as a chauffeur and referee by day (also known as a stay at home mom) and a writer by night. Although she's working on her second novel, she also enjoys writing about real-life matters, such as marriage, parenting and faith because truth can be just as strange and entertaining as fiction. She has a Masters degree in Marriage and Family Therapy, and she loves makeovers of all kinds, especially those of the heart and mind. She lives in California with her family and blogs about life as a recovering perfectionist at www.2square2behip.com.

Kate I. Foley (aka The Magic Violinist) is an author, daydreamer, voracious reader, and fangirl. She writes to survive and will often yell at her characters if they aren't behaving, which is always. It doesn't usually help. She is a contributor to the "Fauxpocalypse" anthology. You can find her at her blog, www.themagicviolinist.blogspot.com.

Marcy McKay is the author of the novel, *Pennies from Burger Heaven*, and the founder of www.MudpieWriting.com. She believes writing is delicious, and messy, and important, so she helps other writers battle their creative monsters on the page. She lives in Texas with her husband and two teens, who all like her. Most of the time.

Claire De Boer is a writer and teacher with a passion for stories and a strong belief in their power to heal and connect us. Her vision is to empower people to become their authentic selves and to live more abundantly using the tool of writing. Visit her blog, The Gift of Writing, www.thegiftofwriting.com to download a free copy of her eBook, *Soul Writing: Why Writing Your Story Could be the Most Important Thing You Ever Do.*

Christine Frazier is a writer, joyous outliner, and compulsive doodler. Above all, she is a lover of literary patterns and their creative applications. Christine is the creator of the www.BetterNovelProject.com, where she deconstructs bestselling novels, one index card at a time.

Ali Luke blogs about writing at www.Aliventures.com, and runs Writers' Huddle, a teaching / community site for writers at all levels. She lives in the UK with her husband and baby daughter. Ali is the author of *Publishing E-Books For Dummies* in Wiley's "For Dummies" series.

Stacy Claflin is a mother by day and an author by, well, very early in the morning. She's currently penning the *The Transformed* Series. Connect with Stacy at her blog, www.StacyClaflin.com.

Andy Mort is a UK-based musician and writer. He is the founder of www.SheepDressedLikeWolves.com, which is a Blog and Podcast aimed at encouraging HSPs and introverts to embrace their creativity and push against the expectations of an often overwhelming world.

Nicole Gulotta is a writer, blogger, content developer, community builder, and good food advocate. She is currently eating her way through Los Angeles, where she lives with her husband and French bulldog. She blogs at, www.EatThisPoem.com.

Chelsea Nenno has a heart for children, traveling, and writing. Chelsea blogs at www.TheChelseaPage.com about life and the lessons she learns daily. Living in Spokane Washington she spends a lot of time outdoors and finds inspiration for life and her writing through the perspectives of friends and family living their stories in front of her.

Josh Irby is a writer who lives in Sarajevo, Bosnia-Herzegovina with his wife and four children. For more than a decade he has worked with university students, helping them tell better stories with their lives. If you come to Sarajevo, you will likely find him in the corner of a local café sipping a macchiato and talking with friends. Visit Josh's blog www.JoshIrby.com

Bryan Hutchinson is the founder of www.PositiveWriter.com and the author of the book *Writer's Doubt: The #1 Enemy of Writing (and What You Can Do About It)*. Bryan is a positive writer and when that doesn't work, he eats chocolate. On his blog and in his books, Bryan helps fellow scribblers overcome doubt and thrive as writers. In his free time, he loves visiting castles with his wife, Joan.

Bonus: The Most Important Goal for Writers

By Bryan Hutchinson (I added this article at the last minute as it is the latest post on *Positive Writer* as of this moment and I think it's a great way to close out this compilation book with a call to action that we might all want to give serious consideration.)

I have a specific goal this year. It's the most important goal I have ever set for myself as a writer, as an entrepreneur, and, quite honestly, as a person. And if I may be so bold, I think, maybe, just maybe, it could be the most important goal you set for yourself, too.

Let's finish what we started.

Several years ago I wrote a short, humorous eBook and gave it away for free. It was a laugh-at-myself sort of book and a lot of people thought it was kind of funny. Over 100,000 people downloaded it. That's quite a few more than I expected.

With that kind of traction I thought it would be a neat idea to write an extended edition, a real, honest-to-goodness, "book" and sell it as a Kindle download. So I spent two years writing it, expanding on the 10 jokes and adding another 10 for good measure. The extended edition is ready to be uploaded to Amazon. But, and this is a big BUT, the book has been ready for over a year already. I'm stuck at the finish line. Stuck in extended hesitation.

Maybe you've been here, too? Maybe you wanted to do something, like, say, write a book, and yet when you're nearly there, nearly complete, getting ever closer to the finish line, you begin to slow down, to stall, to hesitate, and eventually you come to a total stop, you shutdown. Sound familiar? I hope not. But...

How many of us sabotage ourselves from finishing? Or taking the next, critical step to publication? Or shipping? Or whatever your next step might be.

Perhaps you (like me) fear failure and don't want to confront this fear.

My short, free eBook was downloaded over *One – Hundred – Thousand* times. How can I ever hope to compete with that? There's no way I'll ever sell that many copies. No way. Who the hell do I think I am? I mean, really, why should I put myself through the terrible disappointment that is sure to come?

Or perhaps you (like me) fear success and don't want to confront this fear either.

What if I sell more copies? Would my life then change dramatically? What would I write to follow up after such a massive success? Or would I stop writing and retire? This might sound crazy to some, but the possibility of success might actually be scarier than the risk of failure.

Either way, both have caused me to stop right at the finish line. The questions, the doubts, and all of the, "What if's..." Maybe it's better to not follow through? Perhaps it's better to stop and never cross the line? Why did I ever think I could compete with the success (luck?) I had?

If I stop, I won't have to confront my fears, no matter how rational or irrational they might be. Unfortunately, crossing the finish line may be the hardest thing you or I will ever do for our work. If you give it some thought I'm sure you can identify something(s) you started that you stopped for seemingly no reason at all. But there was a reason. Wasn't there?

Do yourself a favor and go back to whatever it was and finish it, don't worry about what will come. Free it. Publish it. Ship it. As they say, what will come will come. And you know what? It will be okay. It's worth it.

"*Whatever it takes to finish things, finish. You will learn more from a glorious failure than you ever will from something you never finished.*"
—Neil Gaiman

There's a tension between success and failure, a place where we feel uncomfortable because we are uncertain. In such moments when we feel like stopping, it helps to remember why we started in the first place. Don't finish for the promise of money or accolades, finish because that's what you do after you start something.

This year my goal is to finish what I started.

Don't you think that's an important goal? Do you have a project you haven't shipped yet? Let's finish what we started this year. Let's do that. What do you say?

How about stopping by the *Positive Writer* blog and let us know in the comments. Or stop by the *Positive Writer* Facebook page: https://www.facebook.com/PositiveWriter.

Stay audacious.

—*Bryan Hutchinson*

The End

"With his trademark humility and honesty, Hutchinson has offered another round of encouragement for writers struggling in the trenches. He puts forth a round of solid advice on ditching the negativity that too often surrounds the writing life and moving forward to embrace the blessings of living a creative lifestyle. His thoughts are solid, practical, and always encouraging."

—**K.M. Weiland** (*Helping Writers Become Authors*)

"I've been a writer for a while, so I didn't expect to learn anything new about writing from this book. But Writer's Doubt showed me the fear still holding me and my writing back from its full potential. Today, I feel free to take risk in a way I wasn't yesterday."

—**Joe Bunting** (*The Write Practice*)

"One of the greatest barriers I see writers face is unrelenting self-doubt, and this book addresses the issue like I've never seen before. By sharing his own story with signature candor, Bryan reminds us that we're not alone. With insightful and practical advice, he hands over the tools we need to face that doubt, overcome it, and create the work we're meant to create."

—**Dana Sitar** (*DIY Writing*)